UPDATED AND EXPANDED

I0065425

Maximizing LinkedIn®

for

BUSINESS GROWTH

A Practical Guide to Building
Your Brand and Driving Results

NEAL SCHAFFER

Maximizing LinkedIn for Business Growth

A Practical Guide to Building Your Brand and Driving Results

Neal Schaffer

© 2024-2025 Neal Schaffer

All rights reserved. No part of this publication may be reproduced, distributed, or transmitted in any form or by any means, including photocopying, recording, or other electronic or mechanical methods, without the prior written permission of the publisher, except in the case of brief quotations embodied in critical reviews and certain other noncommercial uses permitted by copyright law.

Published by PDCA Social
https://nealschaffer.com

ISBN 979-8-9906127-9-2 (ebook)
ISBN 979-8-9940779-0-0 (paperback)
ISBN 979-8-9940779-1-7 (hardcover)
ISBN 979-8-9940779-2-4 (audio)

First edition originally published in August 2024
Second edition, updated and expanded: December 2025

Disclaimer: LinkedIn is a registered trademark of LinkedIn Corporation or its affiliates. The use of the LinkedIn trademark in connection with this book is for educational purposes only and does not imply any affiliation, sponsorship, or endorsement by LinkedIn Corporation or its affiliates.

This book is intended to provide educational information about the subjects discussed. The content provided is for informational purposes only and should not be construed as legal, accounting, or professional advice. The author and publisher are not engaged in providing legal, accounting, or any other professional services. If you require legal advice or other expert help, seek the services of a qualified professional.

The strategies, tips, and tools discussed in this book are based on the author's personal experience and knowledge in the field of digital marketing. Individual circumstances can affect the outcomes discussed, which are not guaranteed. The author and publisher expressly disclaim any warranties, whether express or implied, including, but not limited to, warranties of merchantability, fitness for a particular purpose, and non-infringement. The author and publisher shall not be liable for any losses or damages, including, but not limited to, direct, indirect, incidental, special, or consequential damages arising out of or in connection with the use of this book.

Please note that the digital marketing landscape is constantly developing. While the strategies and insights shared in this book are based on the latest trends and practices at the time of writing, it is essential to stay informed and adapt to recent developments to maintain success. Your use of any information provided in this book is at your own risk, and you should independently verify any information provided herein.

You must obtain the author's and publisher's prior written consent to use any portion of this book for the development, training, or refinement of artificial intelligence or machine learning models, including but not limited to large language models (LLMs).

Other Books by Neal Schaffer

Windmill Networking: Understanding, Leveraging & Maximizing LinkedIn

Maximizing LinkedIn for Sales and Social Media Marketing

Maximize Your Social

The Age of Influence

Digital Threads

Contents

Introduction

LinkedIn has changed dramatically since I wrote my first two books on the platform: *Windmill Networking: Maximizing LinkedIn* and *Maximizing LinkedIn for Sales and Social Media Marketing* (https://nealschaffer.com/maximizinglinkedin). Back then, it was primarily a digital resume and networking tool. Today, it's a powerful engine for building your professional brand, generating leads, creating content, and even attracting new career opportunities.

Over the years, I've helped thousands of professionals, entrepreneurs, and businesses use LinkedIn strategically to grow their visibility, credibility, and revenue. My goal in this book is simple: to give you a clear, proven playbook that works right now, not just what worked five or 10 years ago.

Although it has been less than a year since I originally published this book, the rapid pace of change on LinkedIn, combined with the accelerating impact of AI, made it essential to update and expand this edition. My aim is to future-proof the strategies you'll learn here so they continue to serve you as the platform grows.

The way we use LinkedIn is developing fast. Demographic shifts, the flood of non-professional content, new features, and now the impact of AI have completely changed how we do business on the platform. This book will show you:

- Which older LinkedIn practices still deliver results today.
- The most effective new strategies for building relationships, creating high-impact content, and driving business growth.
- How to position yourself so opportunities come to you instead of chasing them.
- Practical, step-by-step actions you can take to improve your profile, grow your network, and engage with purpose.
- How to adapt your approach to stay ahead as LinkedIn (and the digital landscape) continues to change.

By the time you finish, you'll have a complete system for turning LinkedIn into a business growth engine, tailored to your goals, your industry, and your personal style.

Before we dive in, I want you to know that I've created five exclusive resources to speed up your LinkedIn success—including a 30-day quick start checklist, my personal **ASKNEAL™** AI framework, and a complete content calendar. Whether you're reading this book or just browsing, you can download all five free resources at **https://nealschaffer.com/linkedinresources** to accelerate your growth.

If we're not already connected, I'd love for you to send me a LinkedIn invitation and mention you found me through this book: **https://linkedin.com/in/nealschaffer**.

Disclaimer

I sometimes share the names of tools in this book because I've used them personally, had clients use them, or consider them leaders in the market based on my research and experience. Many of these companies have provided me with gifted access or affiliate arrangements. However, no one has paid to be included here. I recommend them simply because I believe they are the best options available for the strategies I'm teaching.

Chapter 1
LinkedIn Statistics: Understanding the Platform's Impact

L et's first look at LinkedIn by the numbers to understand its power. I include these numbers to share my perspective on LinkedIn to help you gain the most out of reading this book, so please do not skip ahead!

LinkedIn has been around since 2003, about the same time Facebook emerged. That is where the similarities end. While Facebook began as a social network requiring you to have a college email address, LinkedIn grew from the connections of its founding team of professionals. This led to Facebook being a more "open" network of "friends," while LinkedIn continued to use a privacy feature: degrees of connectedness and restrictions on the expansion of networks. This has had several effects on their statistics.

Not the Biggest Social Network, but Highly Influential

Since expanding trusted networks isn't a free-for-all, LinkedIn has stayed much smaller than Facebook. That being said, LinkedIn's membership has slowly grown to around 1.2 billion users worldwide.[1]

The breakdown of users by geography is:

LINKEDIN USERS BY COUNTRY
(MARCH 2025, MILLIONS OF USERS)

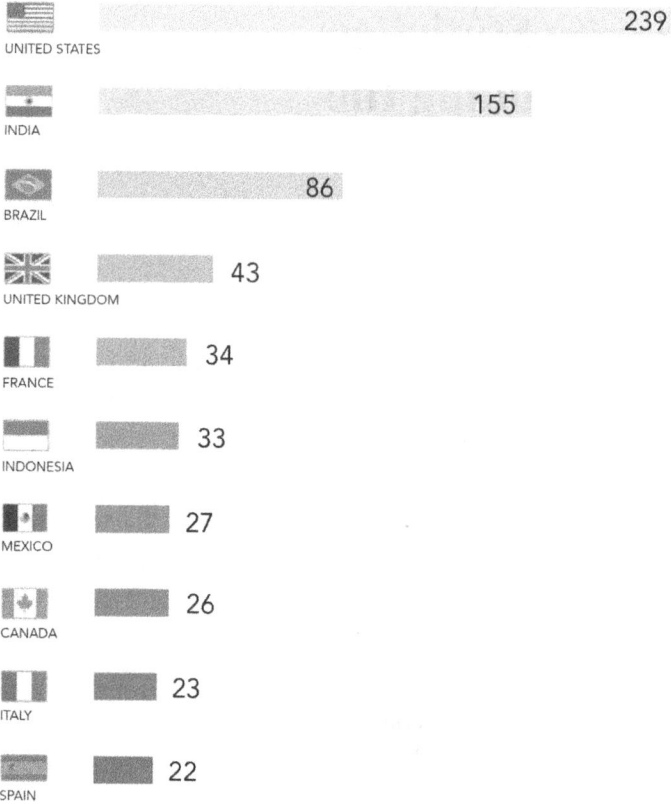

Country	Users (millions)
UNITED STATES	239
INDIA	155
BRAZIL	86
UNITED KINGDOM	43
FRANCE	34
INDONESIA	33
MEXICO	27
CANADA	26
ITALY	23
SPAIN	22

Number of active users in millions

SOURCE: LinkedIn

1 billion users sounds like a lot, but that's in contrast to Facebook's over 3 billion members. Even the newer Instagram already has 2 billion members, and the newest social network, TikTok, has surpassed 1.5 billion members.[2]

What might surprise you, though, is that when compared to Facebook users by country, LinkedIn has more users in the United States, the United Kingdom, and France than Facebook.[3] While Facebook is truly a global platform, LinkedIn continues to have a relevant strength in the United States and parts of Western Europe.

A Platform Focused on Professionals

With that said, LinkedIn is a very special social network. Unlike nearly all the other players, LinkedIn is the only platform that continues to be focused on business and professional networking. It's where professionals go to showcase their personal "brand," promote their companies, and do business.

Traditionally, LinkedIn has been a social network that mainly attracts professionals and businesses who are interested in growing their careers. LinkedIn originally grew to connect professionals with hiring managers and help them find that dream job, but now it has evolved into a broader community that represents far more than that and attracts professionals who look for an outlet for professional networking. Now, 53% of college graduates in the United States are members of LinkedIn.[4]

Decision Makers and Business Leaders

If you're looking to do business with other professionals or project your corporate image where it matters, this is one of the best digital platforms to do so, because four out of five LinkedIn members drive business decisions.[5]

LinkedIn is the most used social media platform among Fortune 500 companies, with 99% of these companies using LinkedIn.[6]

It should then come as no surprise that 80% of B2B leads generated through social media come from LinkedIn.[7]

There are also millions of LinkedIn users who are in positions that may be beneficial to you. Sales professionals have access to corporate buyers, marketers have access to influencers, and we all have access to our peers and potential mentors.

A Wealthy User Base

Did you know that 53% of LinkedIn users in the United States have what is considered a high annual household income, and in a different report, the same 53% of Americans who make more than $100,000 per year use LinkedIn?[8,9] This shows the high level of professionalism and wealth that exists in the LinkedIn demographic.

With LinkedIn users more likely to belong to high-income brackets, you get a feel for its user base, including many who have substantial purchasing power and investment capacity.

LinkedIn's Content Visibility and Organic Reach

What makes LinkedIn especially powerful for the businessperson is the relatively high reach that their content can achieve here. For instance, did you know LinkedIn content receives 15 times more impressions than job postings?[10] This is a sign that not only is LinkedIn not just about jobs, but its members also actively engage with relevant professional content.

Also, compared to other more populous social networks, LinkedIn users don't seem to publish as much as the average user does on a platform like Facebook. This leads to a supply and demand imbalance that is favorable for those LinkedIn users who publish content. This reflects in the average life of a LinkedIn post in the feed, which lasts for 24 hours, exponentially longer than the lifespan of a Facebook post, which is just a little over one hour![11] A former LinkedIn employee has publicly stated that, "LinkedIn's algorithm gives a post a window of reach for about a week."[12] That's quite generous compared to other social networks!

Besides that, LinkedIn consistently ranks as one of the most trusted social media platforms by consumers.[13] LinkedIn users trust the content that they see, and this indirectly can help you become a more trusted authority in your field.

LinkedIn Is a Special Place

LinkedIn stands apart from other social networks, with its exclusive focus on professionals and business leaders. Unlike platforms like Facebook, Instagram, or Twitter X, LinkedIn is not a melting pot of society but a curated community of individuals driven by professional growth, career development, and business opportunities. This distinction creates a fertile ground for meaningful connections, thought leadership, and business development, especially for those who actively publish and engage with content on the platform.

Understanding LinkedIn's unique demographic and strategic advantages as exhibited in these various statistics is the first step toward harnessing its full potential. As we move forward, we'll explore how businesses and professionals are leveraging LinkedIn in innovative ways, unlocking opportunities that can drive real-world success. Let's look into some practical use cases to uncover how you can begin to maximize LinkedIn for your professional and business goals.

Chapter 2
How LinkedIn Is Used
Today for Business

Back in 2011, when I wrote my second book about LinkedIn, *Maximizing LinkedIn for Sales and Social Media Marketing*, I wrote:

"In order to maximize your company's exposure on LinkedIn ... every sales and marketing employee that represents your business needs to have a LinkedIn profile."

Despite its focus on sales and marketing professionals, the book made it clear why having a presence on LinkedIn was important:

"...every employee representing your company on LinkedIn increases the chances that your company will indirectly be found, and the more connected your employees are to others (including each other), the easier it will be for those wanting to contact any of your company employees to do so through their LinkedIn profile."

Fast forward to today, where:

- Social media extends well beyond the sales and marketing departments, thanks to how ubiquitous social media has become in our everyday lives.
- Companies realize their employees are a huge untapped source of brand advocates.
- Social media usage by professionals has become mainstream.

Regardless of what department you're in, it's becoming more likely that you can use LinkedIn as part of your job. Understanding the holistic value that LinkedIn offers businesses is really the first LinkedIn skill that every professional should possess.

As companies have become more involved with LinkedIn, so have individual users. Not only are more professionals now on social media, but they are also consuming and sharing more information fed to them from and with their networks. Companies can take advantage of this trend by having employees share their brand message. After all, the Edelman's Trust Barometer reminds us that employees rank higher in public trust than a firm's PR department, CEO, or founder.[1]

Whether you're receiving internal training on LinkedIn or merely want to make better use of LinkedIn to meet your professional objectives, you'll be glad to know that LinkedIn can help in several ways. Of course, if you are a small business owner or entrepreneur representing your own company, these use-case scenarios should provide you with specific ideas on how to best leverage LinkedIn for your business.

HOW BUSINESSES USE LINKEDIN TODAY

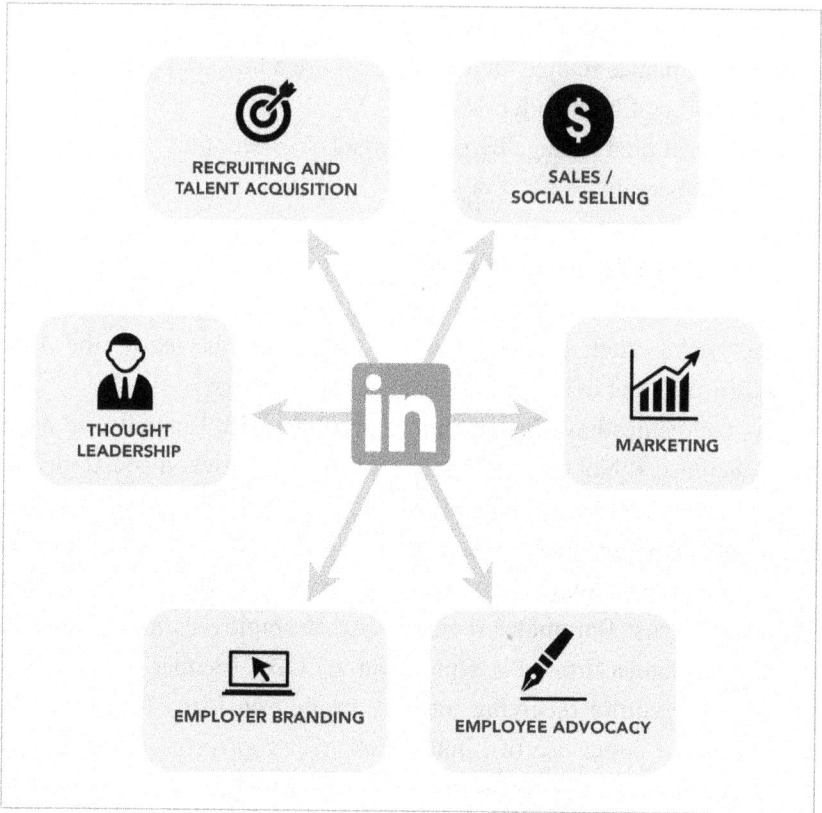

Recruiting and Talent Acquisition

This book aims to help you grow your brand and business, but it is important to note that companies still leverage LinkedIn primarily for recruiting, establishing it as the leading platform. However, once you analyze and re-engineer the recruiting process on LinkedIn, you can see how the same concepts and principles apply to sales and marketing on the platform.

Recruiting is one of the oldest, and still one of the most important, uses of LinkedIn. As the old saying goes: Finding a job isn't about what you know, but who you know. This plays out in two major ways on LinkedIn.

First, a jobseeker can find out who in their network works where. Because many of our college classmates or former colleagues are often part of our LinkedIn networks, it's easy to find connections we may have at a particular company we are targeting. From these "leads," we may find someone who's hiring or talk our way into an informational interview at a friend's company through a warm introduction.

LinkedIn recruitment also works through recruiters. Both corporate HR recruiters and so-called headhunters spend lots of time on LinkedIn. They'll post jobs, search for professionals in certain industries, and reach out in other ways as well.

Additionally, LinkedIn provides companies with unique tools to assist in talent recruitment, including the paid LinkedIn Recruiter product and the ability to publish job postings. On the flip side, LinkedIn also provides job seekers a paid service called LinkedIn Premium Career, which LinkedIn says makes users 43% more likely to receive a message back from a recruiter.[2]

Needless to say, LinkedIn is the best place to look for a career change, but limiting our use of LinkedIn to just that is literally leaving money on the table.

Sales and Social Selling

Social selling, which I define as using social media as part of your sales process, is crucial, especially in B2B contexts, and LinkedIn is a powerful tool for sales professionals to connect with prospects. As with recruiting, it's one of the oldest and most important uses of the network in business.

Arguably, this is one of the better tools in a sales professional's toolkit, especially when selling to other businesses. Here's how it could work for those not familiar with the concept: A software sales representative is looking for potential buyers in the civil engineering field. So, they will look for the buying decision makers in engineering firms, infrastructure contractor firms, and public works departments. They can locate these buyers within their own network, by tapping into personal connections, or by conducting LinkedIn searches. With the people identified and contact information gained, they can connect and engage in introducing their company to a potential sale.

In a less direct approach, someone in sales can use LinkedIn to get to know people in an industry. They might attend trade shows, conferences, and other events, and meticulously add the new contacts whom they meet in person to their LinkedIn professional network. Although these people might not be the decision makers, networking with them on LinkedIn might generate more sales leads, as they might have connections with potential customers. Then, when the time comes, they might depend on mutual contacts to reach out to prospects.

Besides their advanced search, LinkedIn also has paid services to support effective social selling practices such as LinkedIn Sales Navigator and their premium messaging feature, InMail, both of which are part of those subscriptions. I have a dedicated chapter in this book to help you decide whether subscribing to a paid membership makes sense for you.

Marketing

- LinkedIn is a key platform for content marketing, lead generation, and brand visibility, especially for B2B marketers. There are a few different ways that marketers use LinkedIn. First, the simple presence of a company and its leadership on LinkedIn is highly useful: It gives potential consumers and investors a picture of corporate values and personality. Marketers can also carry the corporate branding of a company page.
- However, the two biggest uses of LinkedIn for marketers, which help amplify marketing efforts, are organic content and paid ads.
- Through publishing content on LinkedIn, either through your company page or personal profile, you can influence decision-makers and buyers into learning more about your product or service and, hopefully, converting them. Second,

paid advertising is especially valuable on LinkedIn, where you can target users with sponsored content or messaging ads by job title, function, industry, and more professional targeting options. Here are some statistics to back up the efficiency of LinkedIn Ads, coming straight from LinkedIn:[3]

- Marketers see up to 2x higher conversion rates on LinkedIn.
- Audiences exposed to brand and acquisition messages on LinkedIn are 6x more likely to convert.
- LinkedIn is the top-rated platform for B2B lead generation.

Your Company Page: Supporting Cast, Not the Star

While this book focuses on your personal LinkedIn presence, it's worth addressing LinkedIn Company Pages briefly. Here's the reality: Personal profiles consistently outperform company pages in terms of reach, engagement, and relationship-building. LinkedIn's algorithm, like every other social media site, seems to favor human connections over corporate content, which is why your personal profile should be your primary focus.

Why personal profiles win:

- People connect with people, not companies.
- Personal content gets significantly more engagement than company posts.
- Your personal network trusts your voice more than corporate messaging.
- Individual profiles appear higher in search results.

That said, your company page still matters for social proof. When prospects visit your personal profile, many will click through to see your company. Make sure it exists, looks professional, and occasionally shares relevant content.

My recommendation for entrepreneurs and business owners:

- 90% of your effort: personal profile optimization, networking, and content creation
- 10% of your effort: maintaining a basic company presence

For employees: Engage with and occasionally reshare company content but focus on building your personal brand.

For business owners: Set up your company page; post occasionally, but invest most of your time in your personal profile, where you'll see the real returns.

Your personal profile is where you build relationships, establish trust, and create opportunities. Everything else is the supporting cast.

Employee Advocacy

The recognition of employee advocacy as a powerful tool for amplifying brand messages and increasing reach through trusted voices is growing.

One of the biggest advantages employees have over corporate executives and PR departments when posting messages about the company they work for is their comparative credibility. The reason behind this is straightforward: Those in leadership positions will always present a positive image of a company, even if it's not justified. On the other hand, employees know what things are really like in the office. And if a company makes great products and treats employees like royalty, they'll be happy to brag. Also, public surveys constantly remind us that people trust people like themselves or employees more than businesses, their executives, and their PR/marketing.

As a result, companies are increasingly using their employees as brand advocates. Smart companies will encourage and empower employees to have a LinkedIn account and talk about their jobs through sharing content. This puts a human face on a company and gives potential customers, employees, and investors more good reasons to choose a particular company for their needs. The impact this can have on brand visibility and credibility is huge.

Employer Branding

Somewhat related to employee advocacy but focused on the hiring and retention side, employer branding is how you market your company to desired job seekers. A brilliant way of thinking about it is through this quote:

> *"Every company has a reputation... That reputation is known as your consumer brand, and it can be a powerful if somewhat mysterious force. There's another brand related to your consumer brand that encompasses how you're viewed in the talent market. This is your employer brand, and it lives and breathes in the minds and hearts of your candidates and employees."*—Sarah A. Lybrand and Jen Dewar.[4]

Because LinkedIn is such an important place to source talent, you can imagine how it becomes the most important social network for employer branding. And employer branding is becoming more important because:

- In today's highly competitive job market, it is essential to be known as a good place to work to attract job seekers.
- Without one, it becomes difficult and costly to hire and keep the best employees.
- You need brilliant employees to advance your company, and the best way to find them is to present your company as a fantastic place to work where people spend their time: social media.

As a result, employee advocacy programs are also being strengthened into employer branding programs, collaborating with employees to find new ways to positively promote their brand to potential job seekers and make current employees feel good about their workplace.

Smart companies are also using their LinkedIn Company Page and employee testimonials to build their employer brand.

Thought Leadership

Establishing thought leadership is one of the most effective ways for companies and individuals to differentiate themselves on LinkedIn.

For many higher-level professionals, leadership in their industry is essential to further advancement in their careers. Bank executives want to be seen as financial experts, e-commerce marketers as on top of online retail trends, and consultants as current in their field of expertise. My example is current knowledge of digital and social media marketing trends. Leaders often express their mastery through posting on LinkedIn. Sometimes, they'll even operate a blog or record a podcast. No matter the approach, however, LinkedIn is increasingly the place to find thought leadership in any industry.

Some companies have taken this one step further by implementing thought leadership marketing programs, leveraging employee advocacy efforts, and focusing strategically on their leadership team and other key executives to be seen as the go-to people in their industry.

Publishing insightful content, engaging in discussions, and regularly sharing industry knowledge help businesses and individuals position themselves as thought leaders.

LinkedIn is More than a Job Board

As you can see now, LinkedIn is far more than a mere job-seeking platform; it's a dynamic ecosystem where businesses can thrive, professionals can elevate their personal brands, and thought leaders can shape industry conversations. Whether you're aiming to recruit top talent, drive sales through social selling, or establish your company as a respected authority, LinkedIn offers a robust set of tools to achieve your goals. As we move into the next chapters, you'll discover how to leverage these tools, maximize your presence, and transform your LinkedIn activities into tangible business outcomes. It's time to fully embrace the potential of LinkedIn and unlock the opportunities that await.

Chapter 3
Optimizing Your LinkedIn Profile for Maximum Impact

A s with any other social network, once you have signed up and established an account, LinkedIn will ask you to enter personal information to better develop your profile. Compared to social networks with simpler user profiles, like Instagram or X, LinkedIn will ask you all about your professional and educational background. While some might fear for their privacy, on the contrary, the more information you provide, the easier it will be for you to get back in touch with those from your previous professional experiences and vice versa. This process also adds your keywords to the LinkedIn database, allowing opportunities to come your way.

This is where you need the following mindset to take advantage of what LinkedIn offers:

Your LinkedIn profile is not your resume. It is an inbound marketing tool you can use to create your future and tell your story to attract those you want to engage with.

Remember: Your LinkedIn profile will become your default home page on the internet for your professional brand. Just do a Google search for your name and chances are LinkedIn will be at the top or near the top of the search results. Even for my name, while I have a website, my LinkedIn profile appears as the second result.

GOOGLE SEARCH RESULTS FOR NEAL SCHAFFER

Google

neal schaffer   ✕ 🎤 📷 🔍

Neal Schaffer
Author ⋮   (Overview)   Podcasts

Neal Schaffer
https://nealschaffer.com ⋮

Neal Schaffer

Neal Schaffer: A Fractional CMO, Consultant & Speaker on digital / social media strategy, content marketing, influencer marketing & LinkedIn.

About Us
Neal Schaffer is a leading authority on helping businesses through ...   ›

Blog
Here you can find a directory to all of the latest digital and social ...   ›

Your Digital Marketing Coach
As Your Digital Marketing Coach, I am on a mission to provide you ...   ›

Contact us now
I offer Fractional CMO Consulting to a wide range of companies ...   ›

Global Social Media Speaker ...
Neal Schaffer is a leading social media speaker, author ...   ›

More results from nealschaffer.com »

LinkedIn · Neal 🏅 Schaffer
49.6K+ followers   ⋮

Neal 🏅 Schaffer - NealSchaffer.com

I'm proud to be the Team Manager for one of the premiere soccer clubs in the United States, the Pateadores, headquartered in Costa Mesa, California.

The other thing to note about the importance of your LinkedIn profile is that every action you take on LinkedIn will leave a footprint containing a link that takes others back to your profile. Take a few minutes now to confirm that it represents you well and make a habit of revisiting your profile monthly or quarterly to ensure that your information and branding are still relevant.

Here are my top tips for building a successful LinkedIn profile, starting with what visitors see when they view your profile from the top scrolling down. Please note that while you do not need to use any tools to optimize your profile, a growing number of AI-based tools, which I will introduce in Chapter 10, can help improve your profile.

Add a Branded Cover Photo

Many LinkedIn users take it for granted, but the cover photo that appears at the top of your profile will influence the very first impression that someone has of you. Don't leave the default image in place: Take advantage of the visual branding opportunity that LinkedIn is providing you.

Your cover photo should be something unique to you and reflect your personal branding or company values. It should also be an image that complements your professional photo and supports the messaging of your profile below.

I use this space strategically to promote my new books or whatever I want the world to know I am working on. In a similar way, you can customize your cover image to promote any product, promotion, event, or anything else strategic to you or your business. You can also change it as frequently as you see fit by simply uploading a new image to replace the older one.

MY BRANDED COVER PHOTO

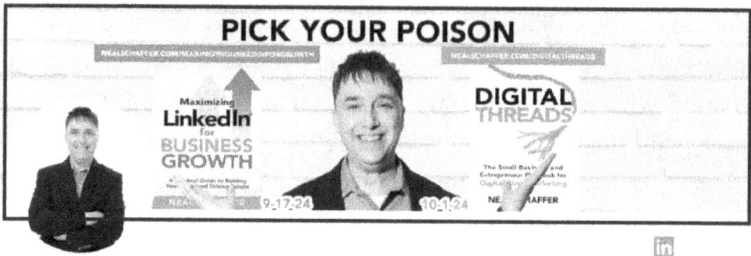

Neal Schaffer ✓ ◀)
I Help Businesses DIY Digital Marketing & Leverage AI to Save Money
and Grow Faster | Fractional CMO | International Keynote Speaker |
University Educator | Award-Winning 6X Author | Fluent Japanese &
Mandarin

NealSchaffer.com

Amherst College

Irvine, California, United States · Contact info
Schedule Time with Me ☐
49,572 followers · 500+ connections

Here is a collection of different branded cover photos to consider from a quick audit of various salespeople in the insurance industry, who often use a combination of corporate, location-based, and personal interest images:

BRANDED COVER PHOTO SAMPLES

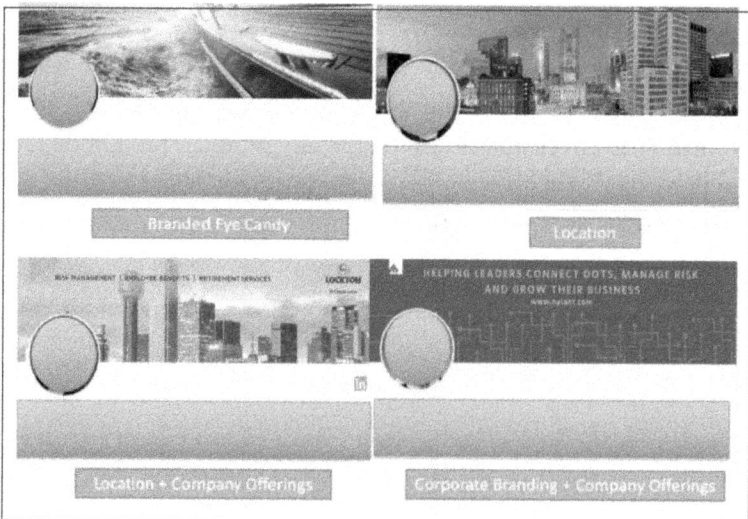

If your company provides you with a corporate cover image, you can certainly use that. However, sharing an image of the city that you live in is a natural, default way of branding yourself with your location, especially if you are in sales and serve a local territory. Of course, if you have a skill, hobby or expertise that you use as part of your branding, like the person in the top left who enjoys sailing and probably taking clients out on her sailboat, it makes sense to use that imagery as part of or to make up your entire cover image.

Use a Professional Photo

The simple act of adding a LinkedIn profile picture makes your profile 21 times more likely to be viewed by others and 36 times more likely to receive a message.[1] Research shows that professional headshots can increase perceived influence by more than 60%, which can directly affect whether people decide to connect, message, or hire you.[2]

Your photo is your digital handshake. It's the first thing people notice, so make it count. Dress appropriately for your industry, whether that's a suit in finance, smart casual in tech, or a polished creative look in design, and choose solid colors that keep the focus on your face. A genuine smile with relaxed eyes will make you seem approachable and trustworthy.

For best results, update your photo every two to three years so it reflects your current appearance, and ensure your face takes up about 60% of the frame, a recommendation straight from LinkedIn's blog.[3] The right image can signal professionalism before you've even said a word.

Create Your Professional Headline

Your professional headline, displayed right under your name on your profile and in search results, is your first (and sometimes only) chance to convince someone to click. If a prospect searches for someone like you, your headline must make it obvious that you're relevant and worth their time.

Think of it as your personal billboard. The wrong headline blends in. The right one stops people mid-scroll.

Let me give you a real example. I once searched LinkedIn for "umbrella insurance" in Orange County, California. The top four results couldn't have been more different:

LINKEDIN SEARCH RESULTS FOR "UMBRELLA INSURANCE"

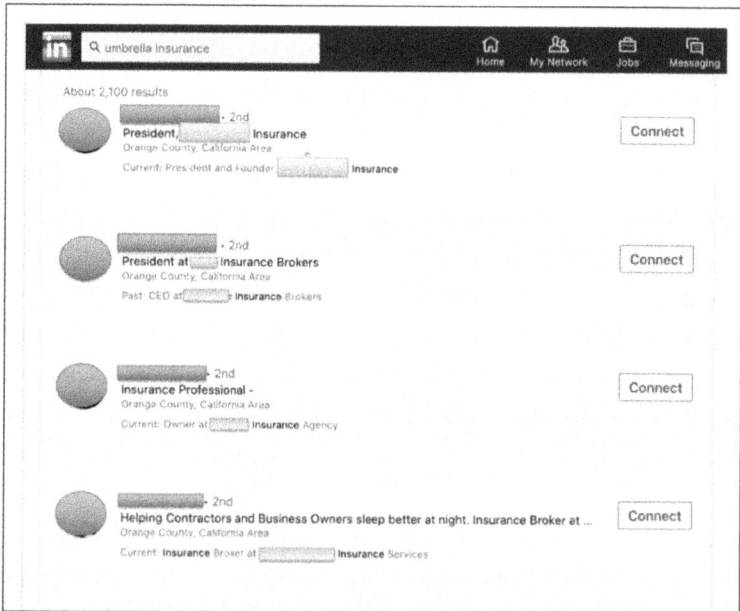

- A president at an insurance company: authoritative but likely too senior for a quick quote.
- A president at an insurance broker: still senior, but the "broker" label hinted at choice and flexibility.
- "Insurance Professional": approachable but generic.
- One that directly called out contractors and business owners: If I were either, that person would get my click first.

The takeaway? The headline that addresses the person you want to attract usually wins.

And here's the good news: you don't have to guess how to do that. There are clear, proven approaches you can follow, and once you know who you're trying to reach, writing a compelling headline becomes much easier. That's why we'll start with clarity before we move into specific formulas.

Step 1: Get Clear on Who You're Talking To

Before you touch your headline, ask:

- Who do I most want to attract?
- What problems or desires do they have?
- What words or phrases would they type into LinkedIn to find someone like me?

Your answers will shape not just the keywords you use (for search visibility) but also the tone (for relevance and connection).

Step 2: Make It Search-Friendly

There's also a search engine optimization (SEO) aspect to your headline. Including relevant keywords can boost your visibility in LinkedIn search results. Think about the terms your ideal client, employer, or partner would type into LinkedIn if they were looking for someone like you. Then, make sure those terms appear naturally in your headline.

You can also experiment with different headlines to see what drives more profile views. LinkedIn analytics make it easy to track this over time.

Step 3: Get Inspired and Apply a Proven Formula

If you're feeling stuck, search on LinkedIn for the role or expertise you want to be found for. You'll see dozens of creative examples that you can adapt. And to save you time, here are 10 proven headline formulas, adapted from both popular LinkedIn trends and expert recommendations, that you can use right now. Each one comes with an example so you can picture it in action.

1. **[Job Title] – Helping X Do Y** – Position yourself as a problem-solver for a specific audience. Example: "Financial Planner: Helping Busy Professionals Retire Early Without Stress"

2. **[Title] at [Company] – Helping [USP]** – Adds credibility while clearly stating your unique value. Example: "Marketing Director at BrightPath – Helping Nonprofits Maximize Donor Engagement"

3. **[Title] | [Company] | [USP]** – A concise, keyword-rich format that works well for formal industries. Example: "VP of Sales | TechNova | Driving 200% Year-over-Year Revenue Growth"

4. **Title + Company + Benefits of Working with You | Keywords | Personal Touch** – Professional yet human. Example: "HR Consultant at TalentEdge | Building Inclusive Cultures That Retain Top Talent | Coffee Enthusiast"

5. **Memorable 3-Word Label + Primary Keywords + Personal Interest/Emoji** – Distinctive and approachable. Example: "Growth Storyteller | Content Strategy & SEO | 📚 Lifelong Learner"

6. **Keyword-Filled Overview + Value Illustration** – Combines what you do with the results you deliver. Example: "B2B SaaS Marketing Expert – Scaling Startups from $1M to $10M ARR"

7. **"I Help" Statement + Tangible Outcome** – Simple, direct, and results-oriented. Example: "I Help Coaches Build High-Ticket Programs That Sell Themselves"

8. **Niche + Specialization + Proof** – Establishes you as the go-to authority in a focused area. Example: "Healthcare Data Analyst Specializing in Predictive Modeling for 12+ Years"

9. **Your Mission Statement in 10 Words or Less** – Purpose-driven and emotionally engaging. Example: "Empowering Small Businesses to Compete and Win in the Digital Age"

10. **Social Proof Hook ("Trusted by…") + What You Do** – Leverages past wins to create instant trust. Example: "Trusted by Fortune 500 Brands to Deliver Breakthrough Social Campaigns"

Remember that your LinkedIn headline is not set in stone. Rotate different versions every few weeks, track profile views and connection requests, and see which resonates most with your target audience. Over time, you'll find the perfect blend of clarity, keyword relevance, and personal branding that makes people want to click.

When you approach your headline this way, it stops being filler text and starts becoming one of your most valuable branding tools on LinkedIn.

Sell Yourself Through Your About Summary

Once someone sees your cover photo, profile photo, and professional head-line, they will next see the About section, which you should think of as your professional summary. Here you will go into detail about how you deliver on the promises of your professional headline and "hook" the reader into wanting to engage with you. Here are my tips for this critical section:

- Always write in the first person to make your words feel more authentic and engaging.
- Consider telling some personal stories about why you do what you do, and what results or impact your work has had (if you can use numbers here, even better). Make note of

key achievements, goals, and personal motivations to create emotional attachments with the reader through storytelling.

- Make sure you break up the text and use lots of white space. Consider using symbols as well to make the text stand out and be visually attractive.
- Add a call to action at the end, such as inviting readers to connect or learn more about your work, and make it easy for them to do so by adding a phone number, email address, website contact form URL, or a combination of these.

Add Featured Content for Visual Impact

If you were to scroll through my profile (https://linkedin.com/in/nealschaffer), under my About section, you would see three prominent visuals promoting my LinkedIn newsletter, a free LinkedIn book (the previous version of this one!), and a YouTube video introducing who I am. This is the Featured profile section, which you must add manually to your profile to take advantage of. When you are editing your profile on a desktop, scrolling down will reveal a top navigation bar that says "More," "Add profile section," and "Open to." Clicking the "Add profile section" and then selecting "Add featured" under "Recommended" will give you access to this powerful visual widget.

This section is great for making your profile dynamic and visually appealing. After adding this section, you should regularly update it with recent work, presentations, or articles that showcase your expertise. Are there specific YouTube videos, PDFs, or links that you would like to send prospects to? Want to feature some work that you are proud of or awards you have received? Is there content that you would like to promote that aligns with your career goals or types of clients you want to attract? This is the place to feature them!

By clicking the + button in this section when editing your profile, you can add the following visuals here that will certainly stop the scroll!

FEATURED CONTENT OPTIONS

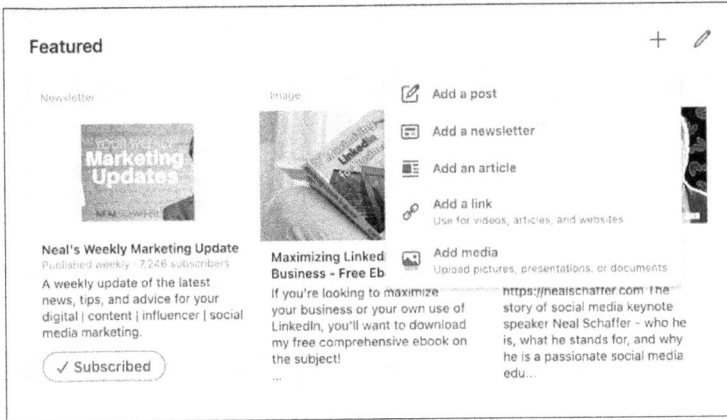

- **Add a post**: To highlight a post that you published as a status update.
- **Add a newsletter**: If you have a newsletter, you can add it here and allow profile viewers to subscribe to it easily, as shown in the image above on the left-hand side.
- **Add an article**: To introduce an article (blog post) that you have published on LinkedIn. Since articles are now considered newsletters, this option only makes sense if you are a newsletter publisher.
- **Add a link**: This is where you would add a link to one of your LinkedIn status updates, an outside blog post or landing page, YouTube video, or even downloadable file.
- **Add media**: You can directly upload a photo, video, PDF, and even a Word or Excel file here!

This is one of the newer and more impactful features you can add to your LinkedIn profile, so make sure you don't miss out on this opportunity to promote your company and/or yourself!

Completely Fill Out the Professional Experience Section

When you've come this far, it seems like an afterthought that you would focus on the experience section, and people often brush over it or only address it minimally. This is a mistake. Not only will you want to talk about your current company and your role within it, but you will also want to go back in history and complete all your work experiences that shape your professional brand. In doing so you are building extra connection points with past colleagues and future prospects who might have worked at or have an affinity for those companies.

Within your current and other relevant companies you have worked for, make sure you detail the roles, responsibilities, and, most importantly, quantifiable achievements you are proud of. Make sure your descriptions are concise yet impactful and highlight how you added value in each role.

Remember, your LinkedIn profile is not about finding a job but about the inbound marketing of the professional asset that is YOU! By only showing your most recent work, you are missing out on potential chances to be contacted by and connect with others.

Don't Forget the Importance of Keywords/SEO

I hinted at this when recommending keywords for your professional headline, but make sure that your profile is easy to search within LinkedIn. After all, when businesses are searching for help, you want to make sure you appear in the search results. Ensure that you naturally integrate any keywords associated with you, your company, your company's products, or your industry within your headline, About section, and experience descriptions to make your profile easy to search within LinkedIn. Make sure you align these keywords with the language that potential clients might use when searching.

In the example search I previously mentioned, only profiles with the term "umbrella insurance" will appear high in those search results. If you fill out your professional experience as I recommend above, you should have plenty of opportunities to include these keywords.

When speaking about the visibility and credibility of your profile, this chapter covers the most critical elements, but it's important to remember that your LinkedIn profile offers even more opportunities to showcase your expertise and personal brand. Sections such as skills, education, certifications, accomplishments, and projects allow you to further enhance your profile with relevant keywords and display your unique value proposition. You should thoughtfully fill out each section to ensure that your profile not only attracts attention but also tells a compelling story about your professional journey. By strategically optimizing these areas, you can maximize your impact and ensure that your profile stands out in searches and impresses those who visit.

Consider Adding a Few Additional Sections

You have now created or optimized the core sections of your LinkedIn profile, but there are more areas that you should consider adding based on your own unique experiences and interests. Anything additional you add here will serve to further differentiate yourself, highlight your unique skills and experiences, and help attract your ideal profile visitor to want to engage with you.

Note that LinkedIn's definition of which sections serve as your "core" ones differs from mine. Selecting the "Add profile section" button when looking at your profile will give you a list of additional sections you can add, separated into three categories: Core, Recommended and Additional. Let's look at your options beyond the sections that I have already mentioned.

Additional "Core" sections you can add are services, career break, and skills. I consider these to be optional and wouldn't lose sleep over them. If you are a provider of services like me, it might be tempting to add your services, but I have yet to see or hear of any business benefits in doing so.

Additional "Recommended" sections include licenses & certifications, projects, courses and recommendations. Recommendations play an important role on LinkedIn, and I have dedicated Chapter 5 to providing you with my advice on them. If you work in a field where having a license or certification is crucial for credibility's sake, add this section to your profile. Courses might be more important if you are earlier in your career or in transition, but showing that you have taken courses on timely topics, such as artificial intelligence, might benefit the personal branding of any LinkedIn profile.

The final "Additional" sections cover an array of topics:

- Volunteer Experience
- Publications
- Patents
- Honors & Awards
- Test Scores
- Languages
- Organizations
- Causes

Obviously, if you hold a patent or have received an important industry honor or award, take advantage and add these additional sections. The same goes for if you speak a foreign language. If you volunteer or are part of a community organization like so many of us, I highly recommend adding these sections as well. They will bring out a different personal and "human" side of you, which will help you better connect with people with similar interests.

Claim Your Public Profile URL

Congratulations! You have completed your LinkedIn profile. While not technically part of your profile, I recommend one more step before proceeding on to the next chapter.

An important step that often gets overlooked, and a great way to make your LinkedIn profile more "branded," is to use a vanity URL, also called a public profile URL. LinkedIn offers a free feature that allows you to select a profile URL, which eliminates the random and automatic address assigned to your account when it was created. For instance, my vanity URL is https://linkedin.com/in/nealschaffer.

Wouldn't you want to have a similar URL that can reflect your personal brand more effectively, is easy to remember and share, and can be added to your business card or email signature?

To access this feature, you'll want to follow the instructions that LinkedIn displays on a dedicated page for, as shown below:[4]

HOW TO CUSTOMIZE YOUR LINKEDIN URL

Desktop

To create or edit your custom public profile URL:

1   Click the (Ⓐ) Me icon at the top of your LinkedIn homepage.

2   Click **View Profile**.

3   On your profile page, click the ✎ **Edit** icon next o **Public profile & URL** on the right pane.

4   Under **Edit your custom URL** on the right pane, click the ✎ **Edit** icon next to your public profile URL.

5   Type or edit the last part of your new custom public profile URL in the text box.

6   Click **Save**.

SOURCE: LINKEDIN

Now that you have optimized your profile to attract the right people and effectively tell your professional story, it's time to build the network that will amplify your LinkedIn success.

Chapter 4
Build Your Network

Once you've gotten your profile set up, it's time to build your LinkedIn empire by establishing a robust network of connections. A strong LinkedIn network is crucial for your success on this social networking platform.

The Importance of Your Network

A "network" on LinkedIn differs from adding friends or gaining followers like you would on other social networks.

One way in which LinkedIn tries to create a safe environment for its users is through its contact limitations. To add someone as a connection, often you must show how you know them. It could be through school, work, or any other social contact.

Why is this important? LinkedIn limits commercial messages to its InMail program, which is a paid offering. LinkedIn regulates your ability to contact people for free based on your network status. First-degree connections are the people you connected to and are the only ones you can message directly for free. Second-degree connections are the connections of your first-degree connections, while third-degree connections are the connections of your second-degree connections.

For second- and third-degree connections, you can only contact them if you're introduced by a first-degree connection or purchase an InMail.

Besides the ability to be in direct touch with more people, every time you connect with someone new, it expands your networking opportunities more than you think. If you were to connect with 50 people who all had 50 first-degree LinkedIn connections, you would be one email or phone call away from being introduced to 2,500 other people through a trusted relationship, assuming no overlaps. Those 2,500 people can introduce you to 125,000 more, assuming they also only have 50 connections apiece, and there is no overlap.

HOW LINKEDIN CONNECTIONS WORK

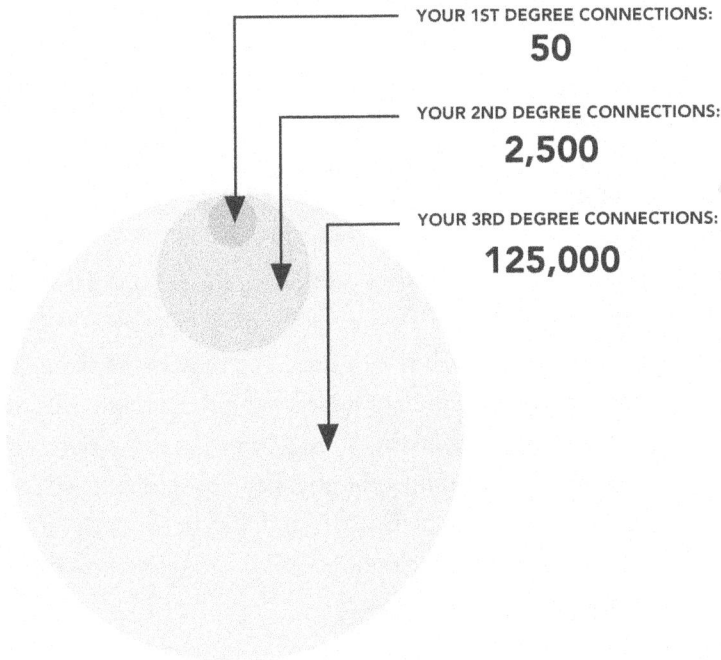

YOUR 1ST DEGREE CONNECTIONS:
50

YOUR 2ND DEGREE CONNECTIONS:
2,500

YOUR 3RD DEGREE CONNECTIONS:
125,000

What does this mean for you? In short, the more first-degree connections you have, the easier it is to reach out to others. There are many potential benefits in doing so, such as access to opportunities, industry insights, and career growth. Whether you're trying to get a job or sell something, it's smart to have a network of people whom you trust as connections.

Understand the Personalized Invite Limitation

Before you enthusiastically begin inviting anyone and everyone to your network, take a step back and understand that sending out a LinkedIn invitation today differs greatly from how the process worked in the past.

I was sending out a few LinkedIn invitations some time ago when a strange message appeared on my screen that said I could no longer add a note or personalize my invitation. LinkedIn has many restrictions that they don't announce, but a search in their help articles confirmed that they currently limit you to five personalized invitations per month.[1] That is, of course, unless you subscribe to a LinkedIn Premium membership, a topic I will cover in Chapter 7.

This doesn't change my advice on how to grow your network, but when you send an invitation to connect with people who you don't know without a personalized message, the advice in Chapter 6: Engaging on LinkedIn: Building Relationships Through Interaction will become even more important. If you want to grow your network faster, you will need to ramp up your engagement so that you can send an invitation without a personal note, and the other party will still remember you and accept. Keep this in mind as you continue reading through this and the following chapters.

Start by Connecting with Who You Know

Remember, LinkedIn encourages you to expand your network with people you already know, and these initial connections will help you build credibility. So, think about not only who you would like to stay in touch with but also people you know who could be helpful to your career or would introduce you to their network.

Here are some ideas of whom to connect with to get you started:

- Colleagues, past and present
- Partners and clients
- Professional association members and other industry peers
- Mentors
- Networking acquaintances
- Classmates
- Friends
- Family

Be Careful Which Connection Requests You Accept

As important as having a network of trusted connections might be, they aren't all created equal. For instance, some people might try to connect solely for solicitation purposes.

This brings up a critical point: LinkedIn is based on the concept of only connecting with people you know and trust. But compared to the past, we are getting to "know" a lot more people through social media. And with more and more fake profiles on LinkedIn, along with people only focused on sales and not professional networking, we are all receiving more LinkedIn invitations than ever.

It should be no surprise, then, that one question I often get asked is, "Which LinkedIn connection requests should I accept?"

Every professional must decide their LinkedIn connection policy. Whether it's only accepting invitations from people you have known for many years or from those who wish to connect and who might add value to your network, you will need to decide on how open or closed you want your LinkedIn network to be. If you're in doubt about a particular invitation you've received, send a message back to the person and ask why they want to connect. If the person doesn't answer or can't do so convincingly, ignore the invitation.

After you become more comfortable expanding your network, you might bypass message sending and simply evaluate potential connections based on their mutual connections, relevance to your industry, and the quality of their content or interactions on LinkedIn, as shown in their activity section. If you feel getting to know them would add value, connect. You can always disconnect later if you don't feel comfortable. In Gen Z lingo, it's not that deep!

How Many LinkedIn Connections Should You Have?

That is another question I am often asked when discussing LinkedIn connections.

A guideline that I give professionals for how many LinkedIn connections they should have is to:

Multiply your age by 10

The logic behind this calculation is: You meet at least 10 new professionals each year, right? I don't expect college students to have 200+ connections upon graduation, but I believe that professionals in their 40s and 50s can and should have connections in the hundreds.

Think about it: Over time, you get to know more people, even if you've been working in the same organization. Each year, your number of real-world contacts grows as you meet more people in your professional and everyday life. These contacts should ideally translate into LinkedIn connections. It's just a matter of taking those email addresses and checking them against LinkedIn's database. Your new real-world contacts who are also on LinkedIn then become new connections.

While I wouldn't recommend this approach for Facebook, where people keep their friends' relationships very personal, LinkedIn is a more open and professional networking arena and therefore perfect for connecting with those you might not go out of your way to "friend" on Facebook.

Here is another thing to consider: Some of the most important assets of your professional life are the people you work with. So what is the upper limit for connections? How many is too many? I'd say you can't have too many connections. After all, "Your Network is Your Net Worth."[2] That being said, while a larger network can increase visibility, it's always important to focus on meaningful, engaged connections. If you're connected to someone who won't respond to your messages, that connection has no value.

The Power of "Hidden Connections of Value"

When I speak about LinkedIn on stage, I like to tell a story that illustrates what I like to call the "hidden connections of value."

Hidden connections of value are connections within your LinkedIn network that you may not immediately realize have the potential to open doors to new opportunities. These connections, when leveraged strategically, can lead to valuable introductions, partnerships, and business opportunities.

For example, I once met someone at a local networking event here in Orange County, California, and we met later for a coffee to see how we could help each other. We connected on LinkedIn to facilitate that meeting. I never ended up meeting that connection afterward, but while speaking in Memphis, Tennessee, her name came up during a conversation. You see, I was showing the audience how, in less than one minute, I could find a VP of marketing who worked at the largest employer there, FedEx, and who could introduce me to that person. It turned out that the person I met locally here in Southern California had a connection to that VP of marketing at FedEx.

In other words, I might be connected to someone you want to get in touch with, and vice versa, which we would only realize if we are both connected and do an advanced person search to discover the "hidden connections of value" that can help connect us.

To discover your hidden connections of value, regularly review your LinkedIn connections, and use LinkedIn's search and filtering tools to identify second-degree connections who might be valuable to your business or career goals. Reach out to your direct connections for a warm introduction. Most people are happy to help.

As you continue to build your LinkedIn network, remember that its true value often lies beneath the surface, waiting to be uncovered. Take the time to explore your connections and use LinkedIn's powerful search features to unlock these hidden gems. By doing so, you'll not only expand your reach but also open a world of possibilities that can help propel your business or career to new heights.

Chapter 5
Establish Credibility Through Recommendations

Everything you do on LinkedIn will lead others to your profile. Show potential hiring managers, business partners, clients and other professionals that you have social proof by displaying recommendations and testimonials from your peers that back up what you say in your profile and help establish immediate credibility with the LinkedIn user viewing your profile.

LinkedIn recommendations are the ultimate form of social proof on that platform. When people look at your profile, you want them to see you as a real, verified professional, and there is no better way to achieve this than through recommendations by peers who can help verify that you have the skills and experience you claim.

What Are LinkedIn Recommendations?

LinkedIn recommendations are testimonials given by your connections that you can display in a dedicated section of your LinkedIn profile. Usually, they're focused on a particular area of your expertise or experience. For instance, mine focuses on public speaking and the success that companies have enjoyed after consulting with me. You should think of LinkedIn recommendations as a less formal version of reference letters.

It's important to note that LinkedIn also has a feature called endorsements. Endorsements are merely a way of giving a "+1" on your skills and backing them up. While they have limited value, make sure you don't confuse the two as they have a vastly different impact on your perceived credibility!

Why Are LinkedIn Recommendations Important?

The biggest reason you should have recommendations on your LinkedIn profile is that it validates your experience and abilities. Think about it this way: Hearing from third parties about your abilities will help a potential customer or employer see your representation of yourself as credible. Recommendations are a way of "proving" your experiences on social media. Then, people don't have to just take your word for it. It is the ultimate in social proof and credibility.

It's also important to note that with so many fake and incomplete LinkedIn profiles that exist, having just a few compelling recommendations from peers in your industry can really set your LinkedIn profile apart.

There are a few scenarios where recommendations can be impactful, such as job hunting, client acquisition, and career advancement. This is because others might compare you to similar professionals. Think about this scenario: I was looking for a local real estate agent and narrowed down my choice to a few. I then went on LinkedIn and found that one agent had a few dozen LinkedIn recommendations, which were authentic and spoke to their strengths, while no other agent had more than a few. Guess which realtor I ended up contacting?

Imagine if you worked in a community or industry where many people knew each other. Having LinkedIn recommendations from some of these people can be extremely impactful if visitors to your LinkedIn profile might recognize them. Instant credibility.

How Should I Source Recommendations?

Knowing the worth of LinkedIn recommendations, you should actively seek them for your profile. Before you ask those in your network for recommendations, I recommend you start by paying it forward and recommending others with whom you have worked in the past. When you write a recommendation, keep it short and impactful: Begin by stating how you know them and the context of your work together, share one or two specific examples of their contributions or results (ideally with measurable outcomes), and close with a clear statement of endorsement. This not only makes your recommendation more authentic and memorable, but it also reflects positively on your own professionalism.

Human nature predicts that some of these connections might also ask you if you'd like to receive recommendations from them. That being said, I would never recommend that you write a recommendation for the sole purpose of receiving one in return.

Over time, you will want to ask for a recommendation after completing a project or at the end of a successful collaboration when the other person feels the most positive about you and your contributions are fresh in their memory.

Here is a template that you can use to ask for recommendations, but make sure that you customize the request based on your relationship and the context of working together.

SAMPLE REQUEST FOR A LINKEDIN RECOMMENDATION

Subject: Request for a LinkedIn Recommendation

Dear [Name],

I hope this message finds you well. It's been some time since we last connected, and I trust everything is going smoothly on your end.

I'm excited to share that I've recently taken on a new role as [title] at [company]. As part of this new chapter, I'm focusing on enhancing my LinkedIn profile to better reflect my professional journey.

Given our past collaboration, I believe a recommendation from you would add significant value to my profile. Your insight into our time working together, such as [briefly mention a specific project or achievement you worked on together], would provide authentic credibility that only a former [boss/manager/client/partner] like you can offer.

If it would be helpful, I can provide you with a summary of our work together or draft a recommendation that you can review and modify as you see fit.

Thank you so much for considering this request. I truly appreciate your time and support. If there's ever anything I can do for you in return, please don't hesitate to reach out.

Warm regards,
[Your Name]

How Many Recommendations Do I Need?

You don't need a lot of recommendations for social proof. LinkedIn used to recommend having at least three to achieve a "complete" profile. If you feel you need a few more, now is the time to reach out to your old managers, colleagues, subordinates, customers, and partners and ask for a recommendation, reminding them of your accomplishments in your request. Don't be shy; many busy professionals that I know prefer that you send them a draft recommendation together with your request, as long as the content is accurate and authentically represents them.

It's important to note that the quality of recommendations you receive will always be more important than the quantity. Try to source a well-rounded set of recommendations from peers, managers, clients, etc. that can provide a more comprehensive view of your abilities and experiences. Whether you write a draft or ask for a recommendation, always remember to bring up specific actions that you took to achieve specific results. Vague recommendations offer little to no value.

Building a powerful collection of LinkedIn recommendations is an ongoing process that adds tremendous value to your professional brand. By thoughtfully collecting and managing your recommendations, you can consistently showcase your strengths and expertise to anyone who views your profile. Remember, these endorsements are more than just words. They are a testament to your impact and capabilities. As you continue to grow in your career, make it a habit to ask for new recommendations to reflect your growing skills and achievements.

Chapter 6
Engaging on LinkedIn: Building Relationships Through Interaction

While establishing your online profile and collecting recommendations is a good start, you need to engage with your connections to reap the most benefits of the platform and gain visibility from your network and beyond. Here are some tips on how to engage with other professionals on LinkedIn.

Engage With Your Network

First, engage with the people in your network; i.e., your first-degree connections. These are people you've connected with personally, and, over time, will also include customers and prospects as you feel more comfortable connecting with them.

An "engagement" is simply an activity that will land you in the most valuable real estate there is on LinkedIn: the notifications section of your connections. While we don't always check our home feeds, we often check our notifications, so any engagement is almost like a digital tap on the shoulder to ensure your connections keep you top of mind.

You can easily do this by simply logging in and checking your LinkedIn homepage daily and liking or commenting on a few posts from your connections that you find interesting. If you want people in your network to remember you, communicate with them regularly.

There are many ways to engage with your network beyond just liking and commenting on their posts. For example, a personalized comment can give you a lot more engagement value than a generic comment, increasing the chances that the content creator, and even one of their followers, might reply to your thoughtful comment.

I will cover the art of LinkedIn content creation in Chapter 9, but if you find a specific post interesting and representative of your own personal branding, you can also share their content while adding your insights in your network.

Finally, besides checking our notifications, we also check our messages, so sending your connections direct messages on LinkedIn when it makes sense can also help deepen the relationships you have with them

When engaging with your key connections, remember that consistency is key to maintaining visibility and strengthening relationships. This is why I have dedicated Chapter 12 near the end of this book to all about creating your own "playbook," which will help you develop a routine rooted in consistency.

Engage with Relevant Content Through Search

Beyond engaging with your immediate network, LinkedIn offers a powerful way to connect with prospects and industry professionals outside your connections through strategic content discovery. Instead of waiting for relevant content to appear in your feed, you can proactively search for conversations that matter to your business or professional goals.

Here's how to do it effectively: Use LinkedIn's search function to find content around specific keywords or topics relevant to your industry. Type your keyword into LinkedIn's search bar and filter the results by "Posts" to see what people are currently discussing about that topic. This gives you access to fresh, active conversations happening right now in your field.

For example, if you're a marketing consultant, you might search for terms like "digital marketing," "content strategy," or "B2B marketing." If you're in real estate, try searching "home buying," "market trends," or your local market area. The key is thinking about the keywords your ideal clients, prospects, or industry peers would be discussing.

This approach allows you to discover new voices in your industry, find prospects who are actively discussing challenges you can solve, and position yourself as a helpful expert by adding value to their conversations. When you engage thoughtfully with content from these searches, you're not just building relationships with the original poster, but also with potentially everyone who sees your insightful comment.

The engagement strategy remains the same as with your network: like thoughtful posts, leave meaningful comments that add genuine value, and look for opportunities to start conversations. By consistently engaging with content found through targeted searches, you'll expand your visibility beyond your immediate network, discover new business opportunities, and establish yourself as an active participant in your industry's conversations.

View Other Profiles

Here's a simple way to get yourself noticed: visit profiles. These can be both inside your network and outside it. Within your network, you can see what your network is accomplishing and identify professional and engagement opportunities.

You should view profiles outside of your network strategically to establish initial connections. These profiles could include those of potential clients and industry leaders. Premium members will see that you visited. If you're trying to establish contact, this can work heavily to your advantage as it can signal interest, lead to mutual connections, or even prompt the other person to check out your profile and engage. Even free members will see some of the people who have visited their profile, so you can apply this strategy broadly to target any LinkedIn user.

Follow Other Profiles

While I focused on connecting with people that you know in the previous chapter, LinkedIn also has a "follow" feature to help you stay engaged with those you want to get to know or simply be inspired by their content. Once you engage and view other profiles, following them is a simple way of ensuring that you see their content in your feed. It is also a "social signal" that you can send them, as new followers also appear in notifications. Who knows? Perhaps after you follow them, they might view your profile and follow or even send you an invitation to connect.

The later introduction of the "follow" button, which you can set in your LinkedIn Settings to be the default instead of "connect," opens the potential to build relationships casually with a group of people beyond your immediate first-degree connections.

Direct Messaging for Engagement

The last way of engaging with someone outside of your network is through direct messaging them. While I mentioned you can message those in your network, you can also do so with LinkedIn users outside of your network to start a conversation.

There are three primary ways to direct message someone you're not connected to:

1. Hope that they are premium members and have enabled their OpenLink messaging feature, which allows them to accept messages regardless of connection status,
2. Send them a personalized invitation request with a message, or
3. Send them an InMail if you have a LinkedIn Premium membership.

While I don't recommend connecting with someone to start a conversation, sending them a message as part of your invitation to connect is a way to get in front of another LinkedIn user. If you want to take this approach to engage, I highly recommend that you mention mutual connections, a recent status update of theirs, or any other commonality that you have with them to break the ice and increase your chances of getting a positive response. Once you connect with them, you can take your time to engage with them as you would with anyone else in your network. However, remember that you can only send five personalized invites per month, so make sure that each one counts!

Which leads us to why LinkedIn created this restriction in the first place: to encourage you to subscribe to a LinkedIn Premium membership, which allows you to bypass the personalized invite restriction and send an InMail regardless of connection status. I will provide my advice on whether you should subscribe to LinkedIn Premium in the next chapter.

This chapter covered a wide range of ways that you can engage with LinkedIn users both inside and outside of your network. Because some of these engagement activities are more impactful than others, you might consider them as an action on an engagement pyramid, with your aim to move from the bottom all the way to the top over time as you engage and develop a relationship with a prospect:

THE LINKEDIN ENGAGEMENT PYRAMID

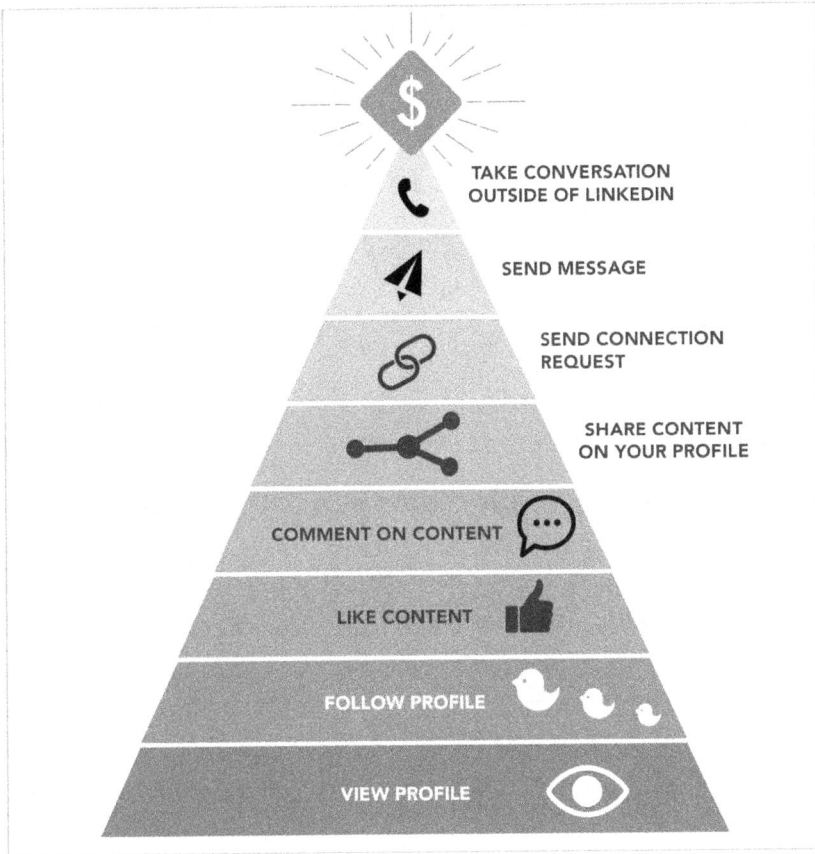

TAKE CONVERSATION OUTSIDE OF LINKEDIN

SEND MESSAGE

SEND CONNECTION REQUEST

SHARE CONTENT ON YOUR PROFILE

COMMENT ON CONTENT

LIKE CONTENT

FOLLOW PROFILE

VIEW PROFILE

As you continue to engage with more people on LinkedIn, remember that meaningful engagement is not a one-time task but a continuous journey. Developing deep rapport with someone takes as long, if not longer, online as it does in real life. Building strong, lasting relationships takes time and effort, but the rewards—expanded networks, increased visibility, and valuable opportunities—are well worth it. Stay consistent, be authentic, and watch as your efforts on LinkedIn transform into long-term professional success.

Chapter 7
LinkedIn for Business:
Free vs. Paid

The first thing I want you to understand is that you don't *have* to pay to succeed on LinkedIn.

LinkedIn's free plan is incredibly powerful. Everything I've shared in this book so far—optimizing your profile, building your network, sourcing recommendations, engaging with and following others—can be done with a free LinkedIn account. Ditto for content creation and publishing, a subject I will cover shortly. In fact, I wrote this entire book assuming you *weren't* paying for LinkedIn.

Most people don't pay for a LinkedIn account, but depending on your goals, there may come a point where a paid LinkedIn subscription makes sense.

For instance, my college student daughter recently asked for my advice on whether she should upgrade to a LinkedIn Premium plan. After realizing that she would need to send over five personalized invites to network and grow connections with her college alumni, I thought it made sense for her to upgrade. As I speak now, though, she has canceled her subscription because she no longer has that immediate need.

That's right: You can become a subscriber for one month and cancel the next one. There is no long-term contract unless you pay for a full year, which I would never recommend you do to maintain flexibility.

With that in mind, let's walk through the decision to subscribe or not together, and I'll share exactly what you get when you invest in LinkedIn's premium features and when I think it's worth it.

In this chapter, I'll walk you through:

- What's available for free (and how to make the most of it)
- When using paid tools *actually* make sense
- What to watch out for so you're not paying for features you don't need

Let's start by understanding what you get with the free version and why it's enough for most people.

What You Can Do for Free on LinkedIn

The free version of LinkedIn gives you access to nearly everything you need to:

- Build your profile
- Connect with people you know (and those you don't)
- Engage with content
- Post your own updates
- Search for people and companies

Most importantly, you can:

- Be discovered via search
- Send connection requests
- Join conversations
- Build visibility

In other words, everything you need to optimize your profile, build your network, meaningfully engage, and publish content. You can absolutely implement most of the framework I outline in this book without ever upgrading.

So when *should* you consider upgrading?

You're Not Paying for Access—You're Paying for Time

The biggest benefit of LinkedIn's paid tools isn't access. It's efficiency. When I talk to sales professionals, entrepreneurs, or consultants trying to build a pipeline through LinkedIn, I always ask the same thing:

Would it be worth $100 a month to save hours of time and get better results?

For many of them, the answer is yes. For them, an upgrade to LinkedIn Premium or Sales Navigator makes sense because they give you:

- **Unlimited browsing and advanced search filters** to help you find the *right* people faster
- **InMail credits**, so you can message people with no need to connect first
- **The Open Profile feature**, which allows anyone with a free account to message you regardless of connection status
- **Profile view history for the past year**—a valuable tool for prospecting and following up with those who visited your profile, yet you don't recall knowing them
- **Access to LinkedIn Learning**, which offers over 20,000 courses to level up your skills
- **A built-in CRM in Sales Navigator**, perfect for tracking leads and staying organized

If you spend even 30 minutes a day on LinkedIn for outreach, research, or engagement, the ROI can add up quickly.

Using InMail Credits Effectively

One of the biggest advantages of upgrading to a paid LinkedIn plan is gaining access to InMail credits. These allow you to message anyone on LinkedIn, even if you're not connected.

InMails can be surprisingly effective. Some people have seen open rates over 85% and click-through rates above 5%, far higher than most email outreach.[1] Shorter is better—messages under 100 words are 50% more likely to get a reply—and personalization is key. A customized subject line alone can lift open rates by 26%, and mentioning a mutual connection or shared affiliation can boost response rates by as much as 27%.

The takeaway? Consider every InMail a valuable and limited opportunity. Target the right people, keep it concise, make it personal, and you'll maximize both your response rates and your return on investment.

Understanding the Plans: Which One (If Any) Should You Choose?

LinkedIn Premium comes in a few flavors (note that LinkedIn often changes the names, features, and prices of these products, so the following is current as of August 2025, but as you know, prices change):

- Premium Career (for job seekers)
- Premium Business (for entrepreneurs and professionals)
- Sales Navigator Core/Advanced (for prospecting and sales)
- Recruiter Lite (for hiring)

Let's ignore Recruiter Lite for now since that's for a very specific and niche audience.

Premium Career

If you're job hunting, Premium Career gives you:

- Who's viewed your profile in the last 365 days
- 5 direct InMail messages (to people you're not connected with)
- Competitive insights on job applications
- Access to LinkedIn Learning

For a short-term job search, it may be worth the investment. But in the long term for business building? Not essential.

Premium Business

This is where a lot of entrepreneurs and business owners get tempted. Premium Business offers all the Premium Career features mentioned above, as well as:

- Unlimited profile searches
- More (15) InMail credits
- Dynamic cover images (to make a stronger visual first impression)
- A custom call-to-action button that is featured across your profile header, posts, and search results
- Unlimited personalized invitations

Here's my opinion: These features likely won't make a big difference. This matters even more if you're not actively contacting people. If you're trying to grow a service-based business and don't have a content strategy or engagement rhythm in place yet, Premium Business isn't a cure-all. Your time is better spent refining your profile and showing up consistently.

What About Sales Navigator?

This is the big one. Sales Navigator is LinkedIn's flagship prospecting tool for enterprise sales departments.

It gives you:

- Access to the Sales Navigator platform, a separate application with advanced search filters to help you better find people and the ability to save leads and accounts to track their activity
- Lead and account recommendations
- 50 InMail messages
- CRM (Salesforce, HubSpot, etc.) integration

If you're in B2B sales and spend hours a day on outreach? It's absolutely a tool worth investing in.

But for most small business owners, consultants, and service providers, Sales Navigator can easily become overkill.

Remember: Most of the success stories in this book—including mine—didn't rely on some sort of automation or paid tools. It came down to clarity, consistency, and relationship-building.

Remember, with a free account you can still:

- Search by job title, industry, and location
- Filter by 1st- or 2nd-degree connections
- Message people in groups you're a part of
- Build your network organically

It's slower, but it's warmer. And that might make the key difference between successful engagement and being ignored.

How to Decide If Paid LinkedIn Is Right for You

To help you visualize this decision process, I've created a simple flow-chart that walks through the key questions you should ask yourself:

SHOULD YOU UPGRADE TO LINKEDIN PREMIUM?
Remember: 85% of users succeed with FREE accounts

Your strategy matters more than your subscription

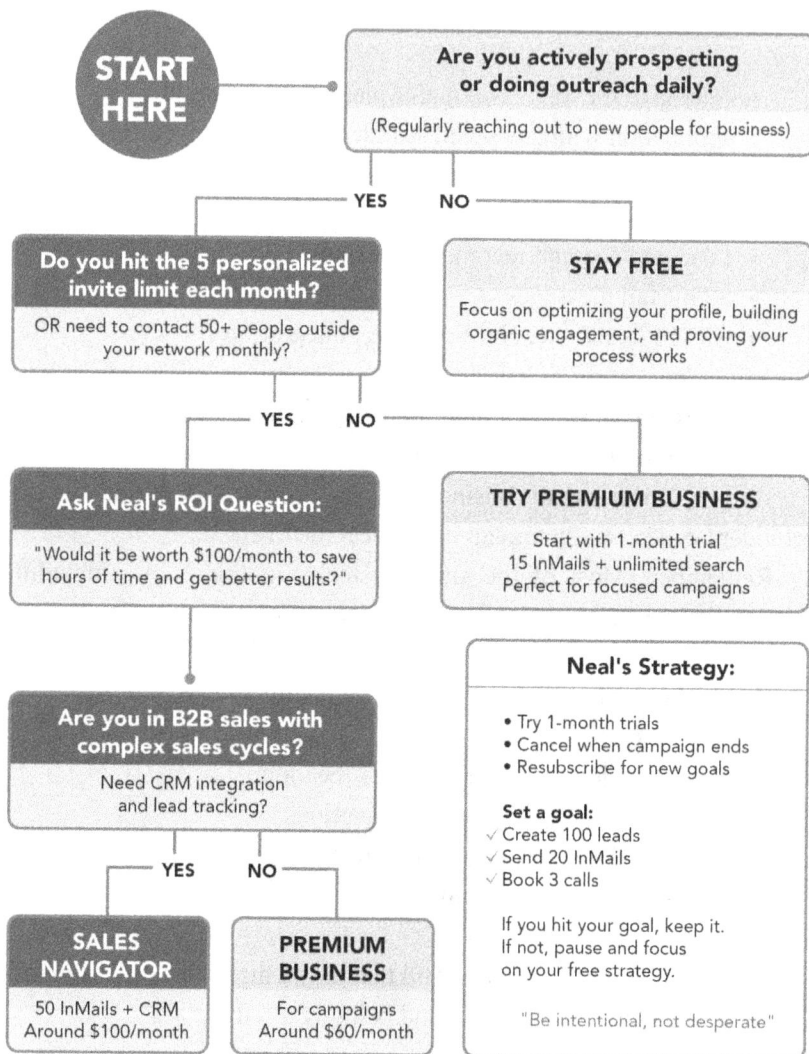

START HERE

Are you actively prospecting or doing outreach daily?
(Regularly reaching out to new people for business)

— YES   NO —

Do you hit the 5 personalized invite limit each month?
OR need to contact 50+ people outside your network monthly?

STAY FREE
Focus on optimizing your profile, building organic engagement, and proving your process works

— YES   NO —

Ask Neal's ROI Question:
"Would it be worth $100/month to save hours of time and get better results?"

TRY PREMIUM BUSINESS
Start with 1-month trial
15 InMails + unlimited search
Perfect for focused campaigns

Are you in B2B sales with complex sales cycles?
Need CRM integration and lead tracking?

— YES   NO —

SALES NAVIGATOR
50 InMails + CRM
Around $100/month

PREMIUM BUSINESS
For campaigns
Around $60/month

Neal's Strategy:

- Try 1-month trials
- Cancel when campaign ends
- Resubscribe for new goals

Set a goal:
✓ Create 100 leads
✓ Send 20 InMails
✓ Book 3 calls

If you hit your goal, keep it. If not, pause and focus on your free strategy.

"Be intentional, not desperate"

Remember: Your strategy matters more than your subscription
Most success stories come from people using FREE accounts

As you can see, the path to Premium isn't automatic—it depends entirely on your specific goals and current LinkedIn activities. Most professionals will find that the free plan serves them well while they build their foundation.

Ask yourself:

- Am I actively prospecting every day?
- Do I need to contact people outside my network at scale?
- Am I hitting search limits regularly?
- Do I need CRM integrations or lead tracking?

If the answer is no to most of those, stick with free.

If you're curious and not sure, try a one-month trial of Premium or Sales Navigator and set a goal:

- Create a list of 100 leads.
- Reach out to 20 of those leads via InMail.
- See if you can book 3 calls.

If you hit your goal, the tool might be worth keeping. The numbers I suggest are arbitrary. The important point is to take meaningful action and measure your output and achievements.

My Take: When I Pay for LinkedIn—And When I Don't

I've used both the Business plan and Sales Navigator at different points in my career. And here's the truth: I don't always keep a subscription running.

Why? Because if I don't have a specific campaign or goal—like launching a book, filling a program, or breaking into a new market—I can still drive results with the free plan. But when I have a focused aim that involves connecting with a lot of new people in a short period, the investment is worth it.

Here's an example: When I was planning outreach for an upcoming speaking tour, I upgraded to Business Premium. It allowed me to see who was viewing my profile, use the advanced search more aggressively, and message potential event organizers more efficiently. I paused the subscription after the campaign ended.

As I write this book, I am once again subscribed to the Premium Business plan. For me, the trigger was the need to become a premium member to send over five personalized invites each month. I want to see everyone who views my profile and determine whether there might be a connection. I want to reach out to my newsletter subscribers on LinkedIn (a topic I will cover shortly) and invite them into my community. So once you get to where you are truly leveraging everything I teach you here, including the following chapters on publishing content and prospecting, then yes, it might be time to think about a premium plan. But until then, there is no rush.

The key to your decision? Be intentional. Don't pay for LinkedIn Premium out of FOMO. Use it when you need it and pause it when you don't.

You Can Still Win Without Paying

LinkedIn's business model makes you feel you're missing out. While LinkedIn has 175 million paid members, they still account for less than 15% of all members.[2] In other words, more than 85% of users are doing just fine with the free plan.

That's why I want to reiterate this again, because it's important: You do *not* need to pay to win on LinkedIn.

In fact, most of the success stories I've seen—including those I feature in my dedicated chapter of case studies in Chapter 13—came from people using only free features. The secret wasn't in the subscription. It was:

- A complete and compelling profile
- A consistent content and engagement strategy
- Thoughtful, personalized outreach
- Organized follow-up (see Chapter 11!)

If you're getting started, stay free. Prove your process. Build your momentum. Then upgrade if it makes strategic sense.

Just remember: your strategy matters more than your subscription. And the best investment you can make in LinkedIn isn't on Premium—it's showing up.

Chapter 8
Prospecting on LinkedIn: Finding and Connecting with Potential Clients

With your LinkedIn profile polished, your network growing, and your engagement in full swing, you're now ready to take the next crucial step: prospecting. I look at prospecting holistically, which isn't limited to just being in a sales role. It could mean looking for and engaging with anyone who will help you meet your professional objective, whether it is hitting a quota or finding a mentor.

In this chapter, we'll explore how to leverage LinkedIn's Advanced Search and other effective techniques to identify, follow, engage, and connect with potential clients and other professionals. By following these best practices, you'll be well on your way to starting meaningful conversations and building valuable business relationships.

All the prospecting advice I will offer here is based on the free plan.

Using LinkedIn's Advanced Search for Targeted Prospecting

Searching LinkedIn for prospects can seem like a daunting task at first. Run a search for "marketing" and you'll get close to 53 million results.[1] Clearly, this isn't an efficient way to find the right person you are looking for.

Instead of banging your head against a wall, combing through irrelevant search results, try using the advanced search filters that LinkedIn provides. For instance, you might look for someone within a particular geographic location. Or you might need to search for someone who has a specific job title. Whatever it is, be as specific as possible and use the following filters that LinkedIn gives every member:

LINKEDIN ADVANCED SEARCH FILTERS

Note: This will appear vertically on the right-hand side of your screen after selecting "All filters" from a people search result. While you don't need to go overboard using all the filters here, you will appreciate the ones that I have found invaluable over time, such as location, current company, industry, and title.

Taking It Further: Precision Prospecting with Boolean Search

Once you've mastered LinkedIn's Advanced Search filters, you can take your targeting to the next level with a lesser known but incredibly powerful tool: Boolean search. Boolean search lets you combine words and symbols in the search bar to narrow or broaden your results in ways the basic filters alone can't. Think of it as writing a custom instruction set for LinkedIn to deliver *exactly* who you want to find.

Here's why it matters: A standard LinkedIn search prioritizes mutual connections and can still show you a lot of irrelevant profiles, even when you apply filters. Boolean search helps you cut through the noise, save time, and build cleaner, more relevant prospect lists without paying for Sales Navigator.

The basic Boolean operators work like this:

- **AND** – Combine terms so both must appear. Example: "content strategist" AND SaaS
- **OR** – Expand your search to include related terms. Example: "VP of Marketing" OR "Head of Marketing"
- **NOT** – Exclude unwanted results. Example: "software engineer" NOT intern
- **Quotation Marks ("")** – Search for an exact phrase. Example: "customer success manager"
- **Parentheses ( )** – Group terms and control order. Example: ("digital marketing" OR "growth marketing") AND B2B

Used well, Boolean search can uncover prospects you'd never find otherwise. For example:

- **Client prospecting:** "CMO" AND ("fintech" OR "blockchain") AND "San Francisco"
- **Partnership outreach:** ("co-founder" OR "managing director") AND "marketing agency"
- **Competitive research:** "marketing analyst" AND "HubSpot"

The key is to start simple and refine your strings over time. If you broaden your search too much, irrelevant results will overwhelm you. Go too narrow, and you may miss great prospects. Experiment, save the searches that work, and keep a running list of your best-performing strings.

Once you've built your targeted list using Boolean search, the real work begins—warming up those prospects before sending a connection request.

Following and Engaging with Prospects Before Connecting

Once you've found someone through a LinkedIn search who you're interested in pitching to, don't go straight to the sales pitch. Doing so will make you seem like you're only interested in the next sale, and it's a good way to get rejected or even blocked from further engagement. While those who engage in cold calling swear by it, most people I know did not join LinkedIn only to be sold to. Instead, demonstrate your interest in who that person is and what they have to say.

Accomplishing this task takes time and implementation of the engagement advice that I provided you in Chapter 6. First, follow their profile (instead of sending them an invitation to connect) on LinkedIn. This will allow the content they post to show up on your feed and give you the opportunity to see what they have to say. Next, engage with their content. This doesn't have to take a lot of time: It could be as simple as posting an emoji reaction, or if you really like a post, sharing it on your profile. When you have something to add, consider commenting.

Before long, your prospect might notice your interest after seeing your name pop up in their notifications. When done right, this will eventually warm them up to your future connection request.

Be Careful About Connecting

Speaking of sending a connection request, before doing so, it's important that you are cautious when sending invites to connect with people you don't know well.

One way LinkedIn regulates its platform is by placing limits on whom you can connect with. For that reason, I recommend that you only connect with someone if you have several mutual connections with. While this might seem counterintuitive, it's one of the better ways to avoid having your account restricted. LinkedIn is strict about people who send a bunch of random invites that get ignored, the biggest reason being to limit spam. By only connecting when you have lots of mutual connections, while there is still a chance that you will get reported, you're limiting the risk to your account. LinkedIn has several types of restrictions that it can place on your ability to send invitations, so it is better to begin cautiously and only rev up your activities after you have seen early successes.[2]

Crafting Personalized Connection Requests

Crafting personalized connection requests is vital to increasing acceptance rates and starting relationships on the right foot. Their limitation in usage of the free product might be the reason you end up paying to play once you realize the absolute importance of personalization.

To avoid setting yourself up for invite failure, take a few minutes to show some common courtesy. A personalized invite should not only include your prospect's name, but also something that either identifies the fact that you've spent the time to read their profile and shows specific interest. For instance, you might say, "Neal, I saw you speak at

Social Media Marketing World this year and loved your talk," or "I loved reading *Digital Threads* and would love to connect with you." This kind of invitation is much more interesting and shows a personal connection.

Compare this approach to the one that I often see receiving an invitation, which looks like this: "Neal, we help agencies like NealSchaffer.com get 10 guaranteed leads a month at a fraction of the cost of hiring a full-time salesperson. Interested in learning more? Let's connect." This type of message ignores the fact that 1) I do not run an agency, 2) NealSchaffer.com is my LinkedIn Company Page name but not my company name, and 3) lead generation for my business is not conducive to the type of cold calling that my relationship-based business converts on.

If you are trying to send out invites that include generalized information, such as [Company Name] [Location] [Industry Name] [Job Title], as part of your invite text, LinkedIn users may sense you are being less authentic and be less likely to accept your invite. Even if they accept and you immediately message them, they will more than likely end up blocking you and reporting you to LinkedIn.

If you don't know where to start with inviting a prospect into your network, here is a simple script that I often use that has proven successful:

"Hey [first name], I am always looking to connect with other [subject/industry] pros to learn from and potentially collaborate with for your consideration. —[your first name]"

Here are some other samples of invitations that I have recently received and accepted to give you some other ideas to base yours on:

- "Hey [first name], noticed you are an [location] business leader. So am I, so I thought we could connect. —[your first name]"
- "Hello [first name], I noticed we are both connected with [mutual connection name] from [mutual connection organization]. I am the [title] of [company], a [location]-based [ecosystem partner name] partner that became

famous for its [famous product]. I would be glad to have
you in my network [first name]."

- "Hi [first name], I'm [your first name], [title] of [company
name] – we [describe company]. I came across your profile
in the [industry] community. As a former [industry title], I'd
love to connect and share insights!"

- "Hi [first name], looks like we're both local and we may
know some of the same people on LinkedIn. Great to meet
you."

Nurturing Relationships Post-Connection

Let's say you followed my advice and someone accepted your invitation request. Just because someone accepted your connection invite
doesn't mean it's time to sell them something. Properly nurturing relationships after connecting is key to converting connections into clients
or meaningful professional relationships.

Instead of going for the sale, keep engaging with their content like
you did before. You've only just built a relationship with this person,
so you don't want to make it look like you connected with them for the
sole purpose of selling to them. Instead, invest in this newfound professional connection. My recommendation is that you do this for at least a
month before you reach out with any type of ask. After all, building
rapport is an important part of the sales process, right? You're also
more likely to be successful if you treat the prospect with respect and
give them time to get to know you better.

With that in mind, your success after connecting will depend on
how you leverage the information from your prospect's profile, their
content, and your previous interactions to start a meaningful conversation. Start by breaking the ice with a thank-you message after connecting. Follow up in a few days or weeks with a personalized message,
perhaps referencing a recent post or shared interest, and look for
opportunities to add value, whether by sharing relevant resources or
inviting them to an event. Remember, relationship-building is a gradual
process, so consistency is key. By engaging thoughtfully and persis-

tently, but not aggressively, you'll lay the groundwork for fruitful business relationships.

One other thing to note here: In the world of B2B sales, it is said that only 5% of people are looking for a solution to a specific problem that they or their company has in a specific quarter timeframe (known as the 95:5 rule).[3] So, 95% of LinkedIn users probably won't benefit from your offering. If you consistently network on LinkedIn and stay top of mind as an expert in your field, you'll be more likely to succeed professionally.

While this chapter provides you with strategies for prospecting and connecting on LinkedIn, the real magic happens in the consistent, thoughtful follow-ups that transform a connection into a lasting professional relationship. As you continue to apply these techniques, you'll find that your LinkedIn network becomes a powerful tool for business growth. The end goal should be to convert these "prospects" into becoming genuine members of your network, creating chances to meet with them online and, ideally, offline.

While prospecting helps you find and connect with the right people, our next step is creating content that makes those same opportunities come to you. Let's explore how consistent publishing transforms you from someone who chases opportunities into someone opportunities seek.

Chapter 9
Creating Content That Resonates on LinkedIn

Before I begin this chapter, you might notice that I do not bring up LinkedIn Groups anywhere else in this book. Many moons ago, LinkedIn Groups were where most engagement on LinkedIn took place. With few professionals possessing the habit of publishing professional content online in the earlier days of LinkedIn, Groups became the virtual water coolers where users would come together to talk about mutual topics of interest and network. Over time, however, LinkedIn Groups became notorious for spammers and self-promoters, and even LinkedIn removed the "Groups" menu item from the top navigation—you now have to dig deeper to even access them.

Fast forward to today, when LinkedIn has evolved into one of the most engaging social media platforms, where professionals from all walks of life share more content than ever before. The news feed, once considered "boring" compared to competing social networks, has evolved into a dynamic space filled with everything from personal selfies to videos, photos, and even "carousel" posts that function as mini e-books. This shift reflects LinkedIn's growing role as a central platform for personal and professional branding.

If you truly want to make a lasting impact on LinkedIn, regularly sharing content is the most effective way to do so. While someone might view your profile once, there is a greater chance that they will engage with you through your content, which isn't limited to a single instance. Posting content on LinkedIn once a week can help keep you top of mind with your network, allowing you to build credibility, strengthen relationships, and potentially attract people interested in your thoughts.

Data shows that less than 1% of LinkedIn users actively publish content regularly.[1] By simply posting your thoughts and sharing ideas a few times a week consistently, you can begin the process of increasingly yielding digital influence on LinkedIn and establishing a robust personal brand.

Publishing Content and Your Personal Branding

As they say on social media, "You are what you tweet." In other words, what content you publish on LinkedIn, whether it be on your profile or content, will help craft the way people who have never met you will view you. Always remember who you are from a professional perspective and why you are on LinkedIn before you publish content. Make sure that each post is meaningful and helps you achieve your branding and professional goals for using the platform.

In the personal branding class I teach at UCLA Extension, I go over 15 distinct elements that help comprise your personal brand. Without going into the details that an upcoming book will reveal (make sure you sign up for my newsletter to get notified when I publish it: https://newsletter.nealschaffer.com), content might just be the most powerful of the 15 elements. Your profile represents a static image of your personal brand, but your content becomes a dynamic representation of it, which can easily reach hundreds, thousands, or even tens of thousands of people who have never met you.

For some, personal branding seems to be an esoteric, hard-to-define topic, so I like to provide the definition attributed to Jeff Bezos, the founder of Amazon:

"Your brand is what other people say about you when you are not in the room."

While we cannot be in full control of what others say about us, we can control the content that we publish to help people who have never met us formulate a perspective on us. This, in essence, is personal branding in action.

Another way to look at personal branding is: With the ubiquitous nature of social media, search engines, and now ChatGPT and other LLMs (large language models), it is easy for anyone to find information about you with just a few clicks. Therefore, it is essential to be aware of your online presence and how others view you.

Personal branding can help you control the narrative about yourself in the best possible light. It can also help you differentiate yourself from the competition.

Understanding Professional and Engagement Content

To help you get started, I'll provide some content ideas and break down the most popular LinkedIn post formats so that you can confidently share content that resonates and gets seen in the algorithm. Most professionals who never got into the habit of regularly posting simply don't know how to get started, so I find it useful in my training and speaking to show the options of what professionals like you are posting regularly. Once you see these, I think it will make it all the easier to decipher what type of content makes sense for you to post consistently.

Let's begin by dividing LinkedIn content into two major types:

1. **Professional content**
2. **Engagement content**

Professional content is all about your professional branding and what you do for a living. Ideally, this type of content:

- Shows your subject matter expertise
- Promotes your professional brand
- Speaks to potential customers, partners, and industry peers
- Supports your company

- Sells your product or service

Engagement content, on the other hand, is all about you as a human being and what makes you different:

- Shows your human side
- Promotes your personal brand
- Speaks to your broader network and connections
- Sells you as a person
- Gets broader engagement, giving your professional content more visibility

This last point is critical to understand. I analyze the results of my LinkedIn content publishing on a weekly basis, and my engagement content, especially the content where I "celebrate" a personal or professional achievement, accompanied by a photo, always outperforms any other pre-planned content of mine.

When talking about social media content, it is easy to get caught up in the "game" of social media. That is why it is important to remember that your authentic human self will always perform best, and those who read your content are also human with genuine feelings.

Content Ideas: Where to Begin?

Now that you know the two main types of content to publish, here are some more specific ideas of what other professionals commonly publish based on my own content audits. Let's begin with professional content ideas:

- **The Repost**: This is by far the easiest content to publish. Go to your company's LinkedIn Company Page, find a recent and relevant post, and then share it, augmenting the content with your own thoughts on the topic.
- **New Position**: The most reach and engagement you will ever get from any post will probably be from this one.

When you add a new position to your Professional Experience, LinkedIn will ask if you would like to share the news with your network. Proceeding forward will create this post. Then you can sit back and watch the likes and comments come flooding in!

- **Hiring**: Considering how many people on LinkedIn are looking for a job, if your company is hiring and you share that information, you might find some in your network who will share your post with their network, expanding its reach.
- **Professional Achievements**: If you recently received an award, a new certification, or another professional achievement, why not share the news with your network?
- **Company Events – Invite**: If your company is hosting an event for which you can invite people, why not share the news with your network? You could share a LinkedIn Event or a link to an external site that has more information.
- **Company Events – Report**: Reporting from a company event, whether it be a professional training or a holiday get-together, gives you an opportunity to post happy photos of yourself with your colleagues. These posts always seem to garner engagement from one's network.
- **Lifestyle / Resourceful**: Do you work in an industry where professionals might be interested in the latest trends and how they might affect their careers or personal lives? While it might not be a fit for everyone, if you work in such an industry, sharing this information can help you help your network.
- **Educating Your Network**: A post similar to the above type but more focused on educating your network regarding your company's products and services and how that information can help them. Professional content will vary from industry to industry, but hopefully the above has planted some seeds for your own content creation. Let's now move on to popular engagement content topics on LinkedIn:

- **Personal Passions**: Do you have a personal passion that is directly or indirectly related to what you do for a living? Even if your hobby doesn't relate to your work, sharing it can show a side of you that might interest your network and serve as a networking vehicle to help find people with a similar passion.
- **Social Causes & Organizations**: Supporting a cause you care about or highlighting your involvement with community organizations can generate significant engagement because it shows your values and human side. Whether it's sharing your company's volunteer day, posting about a charity run you participated in, or advocating for an issue important to your industry, these posts often resonate deeply with your network and attract meaningful conversations.
- **Just Sayin' Hi**: Whether you are traveling, attending a local sporting event, or discovering the latest and greatest restaurant in your town, posts similar to the type you might post on Instagram or Facebook are okay to post on LinkedIn as well. I would rather you showed up in the feed with this type of authentic content than be silent and suffer the opportunity cost in terms of lost engagement.

The above is just a sample of what is possible. If you are already an active publisher of content on other social networks, experimenting with that content on LinkedIn should give you a whole new bucket of content ideas.

Remember, the idea behind engagement content is that it will help you gain more engagement, which will indirectly help you get more reach for your professional content. Let's dig a little deeper into why this is the case by studying LinkedIn's algorithm for determining what to show on each LinkedIn user's news feed.

The LinkedIn Algorithm and Your Content

While you don't need to become a data scientist and decipher LinkedIn's algorithm for choosing which content to display in any newsfeed, it is important to understand a few concepts regarding how and why LinkedIn will display some content and not others. We want to put our best foot forward to get the greatest reach possible from our content publishing.

First, a disclaimer: Neither I nor anyone except the individuals on a need-to-know basis working on the algorithm at LinkedIn knows exactly how the algorithm works. Furthermore, it is always changing. Social media algorithms also include the use of machine learning and artificial intelligence, meaning that those who developed them might not be able to explain why you see one piece of content and not another.

That being said, there are a few commonalities that every social media algorithm, including LinkedIn, has in common:

1. You tend to be shown content more often from people that you are directly connected to. While this is changing as social media feeds become more interest-based (think TikTok) versus relationship-based (think Facebook), LinkedIn will still primarily show you content from your first-degree connections or content from others that your first-degree connections engaged with. The only exception to this is the relatively new Video tab, LinkedIn's "TikTok" experiment.

2. The more you engage with someone's content, the more often that content tends to appear in your feed. This is the key to maintaining mindshare: The more engaging your content is to more people, the more the algorithm will help you and expand your online presence.

3. Algorithms favor different content formats at different times. For instance, Instagram strategically promoted Reels upon launching them over its traditional static

images, as its founder felt that Instagram's future was tied to video. There was a time when we seemed to receive notifications about Facebook Live videos more often than we do now. Perhaps the most obvious one is YouTube promoting its Shorts, and some YouTube content creators finding that Shorts views far outperform their traditional horizontal videos. The same is true for the few who achieved massive viral success with short-form videos on LinkedIn.

The third point is critical to understand because LinkedIn has more content formats than any other social network. When I wrote the first edition of this book just last year, Collaborative Articles were all the rage until LinkedIn discontinued them. Before that, Polls seemed to get the most visibility in the feed, until they didn't. At some point, selfies (Images) became and continue to be very popular. Newsletters, when launched, attract many subscribers at first, and then new subscriber growth tapers off. LinkedIn carousels, which are actually multi-page PDFs and not the same type of "carousel" images that you might see on Instagram, have had periods of time when they received better-than-average visibility.

What I want you to take away from this explanation is that different content formats will always have different priorities in the algorithm at any given time. People also have preferences for which types of content they prefer to consume. If you are targeting executives in their 50s who probably aren't on TikTok to begin with, short-form videos might not be the most effective type of content.

With that in mind, I recommend that you always try to publish in a variety of content formats because you never know which type the algorithm and/or the users you are trying to reach will prefer at any time. While you do not have to publish in every content format that LinkedIn accepts, you will see different results if you can publish regularly in a few different format types. Then you can measure which are most effective for your network and target audience and double down on them over time.

The 12 Different Types of LinkedIn Content

Now that you have a deeper understanding of the LinkedIn algorithm, let's look at the different types of LinkedIn content you can publish. I will focus more deeply on some of the more popular—and easier—content formats afterward.

Below is a complete list of these different types of LinkedIn content. I will follow up the items in bold with additional explanation and advice.

1. **Text-Only** – the oldest and original type of social media content
2. Newsletters – blog post-type content that is published on LinkedIn and any LinkedIn user can subscribe to
3. **Polls** – self-explanatory but one can use them strategically to better understand their network and what they think about issues or trends
4. **Single-Image** – upload an image, like a selfie, together with your commentary
5. **Multi-Image** – upload multiple images for a gallery-like effect, often used when talking about an event or describing an experience
6. Infographic – technically the same as a single-image post, but the image is more like an educational infographic instead of a photographic image
7. **Carousel (PDF)** – a mini e-book that often includes educational content
8. **Vertical (Short-Form) Video** – like what you would see on TikTok and potentially seen in LinkedIn's dedicated Video tab on their mobile app
9. Horizontal Video – traditional YouTube-like video
10. LinkedIn Live – a livestream event, such as a webinar or interview conducted through a third-party streaming tool such as Riverside or StreamYard

11. LinkedIn Events – a post published when creating a LinkedIn Event, which is usually a LinkedIn Live or LinkedIn Audio but can also be any event that you host, whether it be physical or virtual

12. **External Links** – placing a link to a blog post or call to action that leads the user outside of LinkedIn

Now that you know the lay of the land, let's explore best practices for the most popular and recommended content formats to use on LinkedIn in order of ease of posting.

Crafting Text-Only Posts

When you create a post on LinkedIn, it will innocently ask you, "What do you want to talk about?" At the beginning of social media, before short-form videos on TikTok and aspirational images on Instagram, most content published on social media comprised simple thoughts and ideas that people had at the moment. This type of post can still yield engagement, depending on what you wish to share.

While visual content is powerful, text-only posts can also perform well, especially if they're thought-provoking, insightful, or share a personal story. Remember that engaging content on social media is about the message, not just the medium. Check out this text-only post that I did many moons ago and the results it garnered:

TEXT ONLY POSTS CAN BE IMPACTFUL

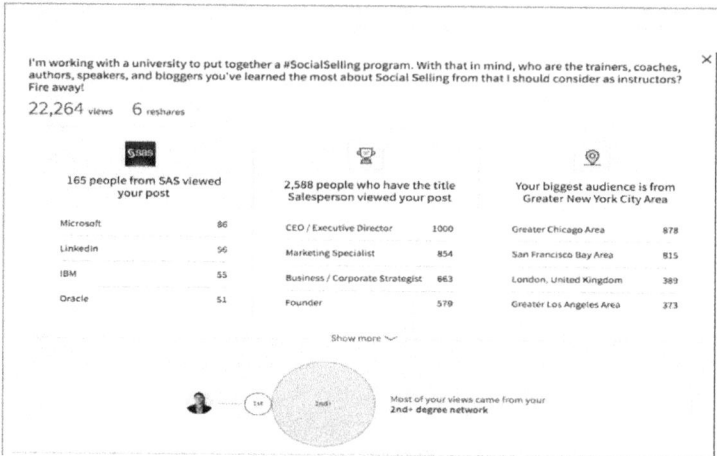

Note that LinkedIn does not show this type of analytics anymore, but I want you to see this so that you understand the people who might see your content, along with the fact that you have a chance of getting a lot of visibility from people not in your immediate network, as I did with the above post.

Here is another example of what a text post could look like as a way of engaging your network with conversation:

SAMPLE TEXT POST

Neal Schaffer · You
I Help Businesses DIY Digital Marketing & Leverage AI to Save Money an...
Book an appointment
1d ·

Goodbye ChatGPT.

Hello Claude (Anthropic)!

Who's with me?

and 23 others   73 comments

Sharing Links

If you can't think of anything to say in a text post, this is the place I would recommend you as a professional start to get into the habit of publishing content on LinkedIn, as it is the easiest to do. The post is ready; all that's left is to include the link and your commentary. Begin by sharing the most useful content from your company website with your network. If it's already on your LinkedIn Company Page, simply share the post to make publishing easier and to be a good corporate citizen.

You can also share content from other websites that you visit if you think it would interest your network. Unfortunately, though, compared to the other formats I will introduce, this type of content will get you the least amount of visibility simply because LinkedIn, like every other social networking site, doesn't want its users to leave its platform. That is why, as shown in my sample below, give as much context to what you are sharing as possible to provide value and showcase your personal brand—without LinkedIn users needing to leave the site. This is the concept of Platform Authentic Content that I introduce in *Digital Threads* (https://nealschaffer.com/digitalthreadsamazon), which is central to your success in social media marketing today.

SAMPLE LINK POST

Neal 🎙 Schaffer 🔗 · You
I Help Businesses DIY Digital Marketing & Leverage AI to Save M...
Book an appointment
3mo · 🌐

Keyword research is the cornerstone of any solid SEO strategy—but with so many tools out there, choosing the right one can feel overwhelming.

In my latest guide, I break down the 15 Best Keyword Research Tools for 2025 (Free + Paid), detailing standout features, pricing, and best-use scenarios to help you elevate your SEO game.

I've been in the digital marketing trenches long enough to know that the right tool can transform your strategy.

Here's a sneak peek at the first five tools I'm highlighting:

• Google Keyword Planner:

• Semrush:

• Ahrefs Keywords Explorer:

•AnswerThePublic:

• Google Search Console:

Curious to see all 15 tools and discover which one is best for your needs?

Head over to my blog to dive deeper into these solutions and take your keyword strategy to the next level:

https://lnkd.in/gb64DjJa

The 15 Best Keyword Research Tools in 2025 (Free + Paid)
nealschaffer.com

👍❤️👏 ▓▓▓▓▓▓ and 13 others   1 comment

One "hack" that will improve the visibility of your link-based content is, instead of including the link in your post, include an image from the post. This means that you are technically publishing an image instead of a link, improving the chances that the algorithm will favor your content. While many suggest you include the link in a comment and note it in your post to encourage readers to visit the intended URL, you can also simply include the link in the original caption. At a minimum, your post will have more visibility in the newsfeed when compared to the small thumbnail image attached to the above link post, as shown in the screenshot below.

SAMPLE LINK POST PUBLISHED AS AN IMAGE

Neal Schaffer · You
I Help Businesses DIY Digital Marketing & Leverage AI to Save M...
Book an appointment
3w · 🌐

A proper audit is one of the highest ROI activities you can do — yet it's the most neglected.

☑ It shows you which channels drain your budget.
☑ It shows you which posts actually drive results (not just vanity likes).
☑ It shows you exactly where you're missing opportunities your competitors are capitalizing on right now.

I just published a complete Social Media Audit Checklist for marketing pros who want to stop guessing and start optimizing.

It covers:

— How to do a full inventory (and why you'll find dead profiles you forgot existed)
— How to spot inconsistencies that confuse your audience
— How to benchmark your performance — and know if you're ahead or falling behind
— How to turn audit findings into an action plan that actually grows your business

If you're serious about making your social media work smarter in the next quarter, this is for you.

👉 Ready to stop hoping and start auditing?

Here's the step-by-step checklist: https://lnkd.in/gUuagddy

Social Media Audit Benefits & Value   ⚡NEALSCHAFFER

👏❤ [████████] and 16 others   14 comments

Posting Images (Selfies)

Some older LinkedIn users may scoff at this idea, but with newer generations converging on LinkedIn, it has become quite common to see a selfie or two in the news feed on any day. The trick is not to just post a selfie but to share some interesting content with it as well. It could be your thoughts of the day, an experience you had on a recent client visit, or perhaps a response to a question that you often receive. If you don't want to post a selfie, the next best thing is photos from a business (or personal) event that you went to or holiday-related images, which often get decent engagement but not as much as adding a more personal touch with a personal photo.

The best "selfie" posts are photos of you in your natural work environment, even if it isn't technically a selfie, like my example below:

SAMPLE SELFIE POST

Neal ⬤ Schaffer 🔲 · You   ···
I Help Businesses DIY Digital Marketing & Leverage AI to Save M...
Book an appointment
8mo · 🌐

New semester teaching Personal Branding: How to Become an Influencer at UCLA Extension has begun!

I have had a LOT of fun both developing content for this course and engaging with students who come from all walks of life and represent 7 different countries!

I am looking forward to developing this content into a book - coming soon!

Yesterday we talked about the elements of personal branding and what are its most important attributes.

This is the order in which my class voted:

1) Authenticity

2) Consistency

3) Expertise (Niche)

4) Purpose (The Why)

5) Visibility (often but not limited to social media and often but not limited to publishing content)

6) Values

7) Your Story / Storytelling

8) Differentiation

9) Community / Networking

10) Perspective / Point of View

◯◉◯ 53   18 comments

Publishing Multi-Image Photo Galleries

When you share multiple photos in a single LinkedIn post, they can appear as an attractive collage, as in the sample post below. Some popular occasions for posting multiple photos could be a conference or professional event you attended, a client visit or meeting, or a general business trip. Obviously, you also want to add commentary, like you would in a selfie post.

SAMPLE PHOTO GALLERY POST

Neal ⚡ Schaffer 🔗 · You
I Help Businesses DIY Digital Marketing & Leverage AI to Save M...
Book an appointment
9mo · 🌐

It has been such an honor to be teaching at Rutgers Business School Executive Education since 2012.

Just got back from recording my latest module, The Role of Social Media in Marketing and Branding, which is part of the Mini-MBA in Brand Development & Marketing Communications.

While the classes I have been teaching at Rutgers Business School have changed over time, I am always impressed by the calibre of programs they offer and educators they attract.

If you are looking for executive education, check out Rutgers - and Go Scarlet Knights!

#rutgersuniversity #executiveeducation #branddevelopment #marketingcommunications #branding

Uploading LinkedIn Carousels

Prominently featured at various times in the LinkedIn news feed, the LinkedIn carousel post is one of the newer types of content. On platforms like Instagram, a "carousel post" typically refers to a post with multiple photos, similar to a photo gallery. However, on LinkedIn, a carousel post is actually a PDF that's uploaded to the platform, becoming swipe-able so users can navigate through the pages by swiping left or right on mobile devices or by clicking arrows on a computer.

Any content format that keeps users on the platform engaging with your profile for longer will always perform well in the algorithm, and the LinkedIn carousel post is no exception. You can easily create these square or portrait-sized PDFs using software like Adobe Express or Canva. If you already have a blog post, presentation, or thoughts on a subject, you can simply design a five- to 10-page PDF where each idea or step graphically displays on a page in an attractive, user-friendly format. After creating the PDF, simply upload it as a document, add a title, describe the document in the post text, and publish.

Below is an example of one that I created to get a feel for how they appear after publication:

LINKEDIN CAROUSEL POST EXAMPLE

Neal Schaffer · You
I Help Businesses DIY Digital Marketing & Leverage AI to Save M...
Book an appointment
4w · 🌐

Marketers want AI to be the magic bullet. But the truth?
Most of us are using it wrong — and wasting time we don't have.
I've spent this year helping brands and creators who thought AI would fix everything.
What actually happened? It just made bad work faster.
If you feel like you're spinning your wheels — you're not alone.

Below, I'm breaking down 5 hard truths about AI that too many marketers ignore.

Read these. Save them.

And use AI the right way — as a tool, not a crutch.
Swipe through →   Then tell me: which truth hits home for you?
And what other truths did I miss?

🚀 Follow @NealSchaffer for real-talk AI marketing that actually works.

5 HARD TRUTHS
ABOUT
AI IN MARKETING

Marketers keep ignoring these.

@NealSchaffer   →

Creating LinkedIn Polls

At one point, LinkedIn users saw their news feeds flooded with polls, but LinkedIn has since scaled back their prominence. That being said, they can still be a powerful engagement vehicle when done right. I wouldn't post polls too frequently as many have seen too many of them, but if the question and answers are so interesting that people will want to know how others voted, you could certainly consider posting a poll on a monthly basis.

LINKEDIN POLL EXAMPLE

Neal 🖊 Schaffer · You   • • •
Author, The Age of Influence | Fractional CMO | Digital / Social Media / C...
1d · 🌐

Hi friends, I am working on developing my first cohort-based learning program and I'd appreciate your input as to what you would be most interested to learn about:

1) Influencer Marketing Strategy
2) SEO-Optimized Content Library
3) LinkedIn Profile Optimization

Thank you!

#influencermarketing #seo #linkedintips

If you had to choose between one of these cohort learning courses, which would interest you the most?
You can see how people vote. Learn more

Influencer Marketing Strategy	40%
SEO-Optimized Content Library	37%
LinkedIn Profile Optimization	23%

143 votes · 5d left · Hide results

🔵🟣 16

Uploading Short-Form Videos

With the popularity of Instagram Reels and TikTok, the thought of uploading a similar type of video to LinkedIn is not as crazy as it would have sounded a few years ago. Not everyone is publishing video content, but if you are posting videos to other social networks, there's no better way to engage emotionally with your network than through video on LinkedIn. You could cover similar topics as you would in the selfie post described above, or you could interview a business partner or industry professional. I upload the same professional videos on LinkedIn as I do on TikTok, Instagram Reels, and YouTube Shorts, as you can see below!

LINKEDIN SHORT-FORM VIDEO EXAMPLE

Neal Schaffer · You   ...
I Help Businesses DIY Digital Marketing & Leverage AI to Save M...
Book an appointment
1mo · 🌐

7 must-read business books—and the tool I used to make this video pop.

From AI to SEO to social media, these picks will level up your summer reading and your marketing.

Featuring books from Phil Pallen, Eric Ries, Niraj Kapur, Peg Fitzpatrick, Phil Treagus-Evans, Jason Hennessey and yours truly 😎

Created with Adobe Express 😍 Try it out at adobe.com/express and then let me know how it helps YOU stay on-trend and stand out visually!

#AdobeExpressAmbassadors #Ad #SummerSocialHacks
#BusinessBooks #AdobeExpress #ContentCreation

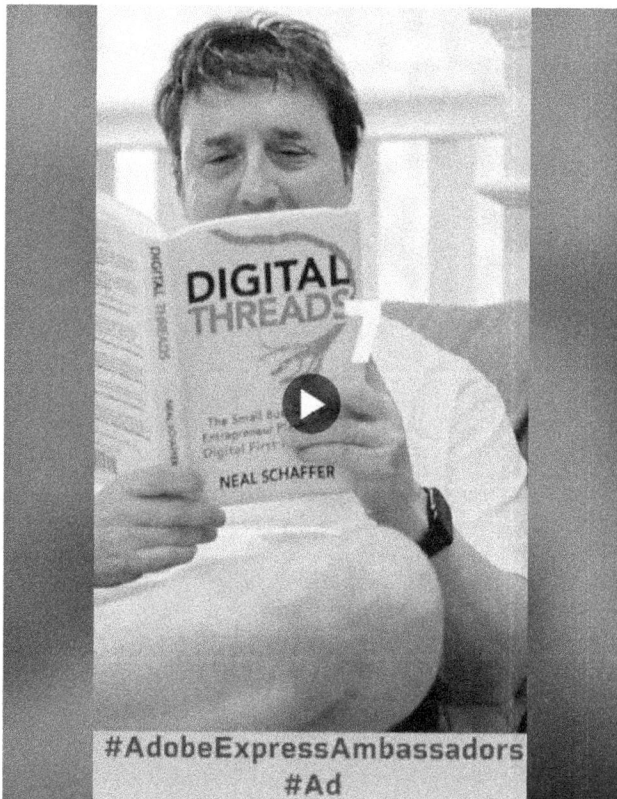

These are the seven most popular and easiest types of content to publish on your personal feed. Obviously, if you are a blogger or already publish a regular newsletter, publishing a LinkedIn Newsletter will be easy. The same goes for podcasters, who can now livestream their events using the LinkedIn Live format. Assuming that 99% of those reading this book are neither bloggers nor podcasters (or YouTubers, for that matter), sticking to these seven types of content should be sufficient to help you reach your goals on LinkedIn.

Using User-Generated Content (UGC)

Now that you understand the major content formats and things you can talk about, you are ready to begin publishing regularly. That being said, I also want to remind you that you don't have to create all your content.

In my latest book, *Digital Threads*, I emphasize that publishing user-generated content—content other social media users create about you or your product—is the most powerful type you can share. Why? The fact that someone else is talking about you gives you credibility that you can't get through your own voice, and it also means one less piece of content for you to create!

The challenge is in generating this type of content.

If you think about it, people outside your organization or immediate team, such as customers, clients, or even other professionals in your network, create UGC for professionals. Therefore, you might already have UGC that you can repurpose and use as a type of content on LinkedIn today. Here is what UGC for professionals would look like:

1. **Customer Testimonials**: Share quotes or stories from clients who have benefited from your services or products. This not only builds credibility but also fosters trust within your network.

2. **Case Studies from Clients**: Ask your clients to share their success stories on LinkedIn and tag you or your company. You can then reshare these posts with your network, highlighting the impact of your work.

3. **Reviews and Recommendations**: Encourage your connections or clients to leave recommendations on your LinkedIn profile. You can periodically share these as posts, thanking them for their support.

4. **Content Created by Others Featuring You**: If someone mentions you or your work in a blog post, article, or video, share that content on your LinkedIn feed with a note of gratitude.

5. **Client-Created Visuals or Videos**: Share visuals or videos that your clients have created using your products or services. This is especially effective if the content is creative, demonstrating real-world applications of what you offer.

A Strategic Approach to Generating Professional UGC: Podcast Appearances

One of the most effective ways I've found to generate high-quality user-generated content as a professional is through podcast appearances. When you're interviewed on a podcast, you automatically gain several UGC benefits: The host's introduction lends immediate credibility and social proof, the episode becomes shareable content, and many podcasts now record video interviews, giving you short-form video clips perfect for LinkedIn posts.

The beauty of podcast UGC is that the host is essentially creating content that positions you as an expert to their audience. When you share clips or quotes from your interview, you're not self-promoting—you're sharing third-party validation of your expertise.

If you're interested in pursuing podcast appearances, I recommend checking out Podmatch (https://nealschaffer.com/podmatch), a community that connects podcasters with potential guests. It's a platform I've used successfully to jumpstart podcast appearances and build relationships with hosts looking for experts in various fields.

UGC Best Practices and Permissions

UGC is undoubtedly the hardest and most valuable type of content to generate. With some strategic thinking on how to have others you serve generate content on your behalf, though, you will uncover opportunities in the future, however few or many they may be. Once your personal brand grows and you have opportunities to be interviewed on podcasts and the like, these opportunities will grow.

I was going to publish an example here from an appearance I made on my friend Amy Wood's excellent *The Content 10X Podcast*, which I highly recommend you subscribe to.[2] She referred to me as someone for whom there is no one better to speak to about influencer marketing when sharing the published podcast episode on LinkedIn.[3] When I reshare that LinkedIn newsletter article on LinkedIn, it becomes an example of sharing user-generated content on my profile that I was not the original creator of.

I didn't publish that post here as a reminder that unless someone published a public social media post you can easily share on that platform, you don't necessarily have the right to publish it on your own profile (or in this case, a book). This applies to companies publishing user-generated content as well: They should ask permission from the content creator to publish someone else's content on their company profile. The same goes for you: If someone wrote you a recommendation, gave you a testimonial, or created content not published on a public platform like social media, it is always in your best interest to request permission before publishing that content on your profile.

There are other types of content that you might see in your feed, but the above are the easiest ways to make an impact with content. Publishing content on a regular basis is not a simple thing to do, but once you get into the habit of doing it, it becomes easier over time. My suggestion is to always start slow, even at a once-a-month pace, but leverage opportunities to capture photos and videos that you can post later should you feel comfortable doing so.

Creating great content consistently can feel overwhelming—especially when you're trying to maintain authenticity while staying productive. In our next chapter, we'll explore how AI can become your content creation assistant without sacrificing your unique voice.

Chapter 10
Leveraging AI to Enhance Your LinkedIn

With the emergence of ChatGPT and generative AI, most, if not all businesses, are already using, or at least trying to figure out how to best use, artificial intelligence in their organizations. The same goes for people like you and me. After all, they say that we won't lose our jobs to AI but could to someone who can use AI better than us.

Fortunately, there are many ways to use AI to enhance your LinkedIn experience, which I will introduce next for your consideration. Similar to how you do not need to pay for a premium account to take advantage of all my advice in this book, you also don't need to use AI to be successful on LinkedIn. However, knowledge is power, and understanding what technology and tools are available to you is critical. Whether you take advantage of it is up to you.

One important note regarding the use of AI on LinkedIn: I will not be talking about the various automation tools that exist that often land people in "LinkedIn jail," and sometimes ban them from accessing the platform for life. LinkedIn is too critical a platform to risk being kicked off of. These tools are primarily for various types of content creation and will not perform the automations that put your account at risk.

I should point out here that while I didn't mention it in Chapter 7 while introducing LinkedIn's paid plans, those plans also grant access to LinkedIn's internal AI tools, which can draft LinkedIn messages, as well as create a first draft of any content you would like to share. The fact that LinkedIn is offering AI tools as part of its premium plans should validate AI usage on LinkedIn! The reason I did not mention this feature earlier is that I recommend using your own personal LLM (ChatGPT, Google Gemini, Claude, etc.) instead of LinkedIn's. I will discuss why shortly.

So what is possible when leveraging AI for LinkedIn?

THE DIFFERENT WAYS AI CAN BE USED ON LINKEDIN

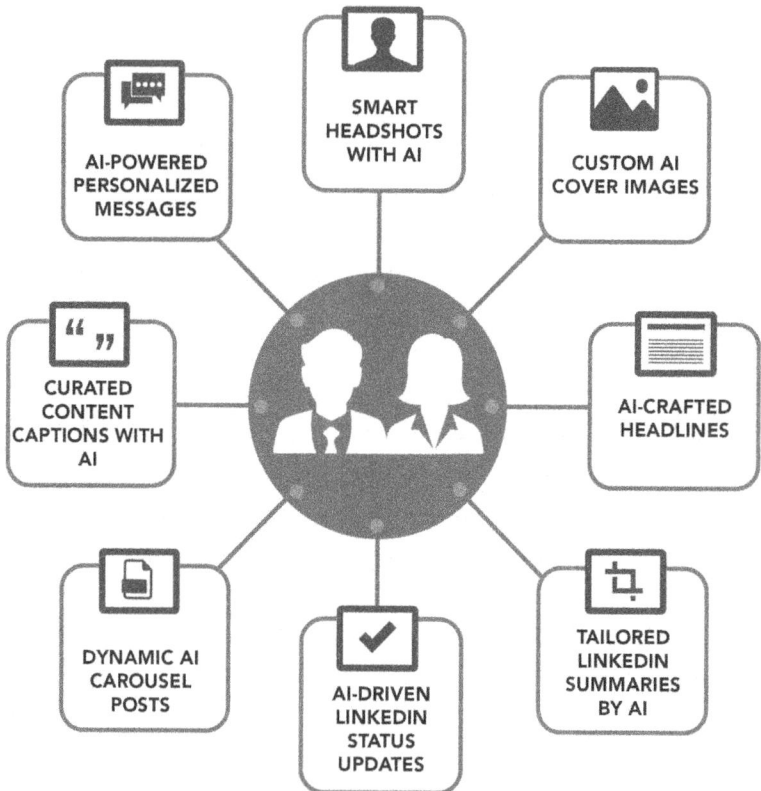

Unlocking LinkedIn's Potential with ChatGPT

When ChatGPT first appeared, it ushered in a new generation of digital marketing tools that tapped into ChatGPT and other large language models (LLMs) to provide useful content to businesses. I started using various third-party tools to eliminate the need to learn how to create the right prompt to get the best answer to my query, making it that much easier to harness the power of generative AI. While I still use some of these AI tools for LinkedIn and other aspects of digital marketing, I most frequently use ChatGPT and customize the response I would like to receive. That is why any section on AI must begin with ChatGPT, as it is a versatile tool you can use to streamline many aspects of your LinkedIn presence and enhance your LinkedIn experience, from content creation to profile optimization and engagement strategies.

If you use another LLM, such as Google Gemini, Claude, Grok, etc., don't worry. The advice here applies to any LLM. I only use ChatGPT as a reference, but you should be able to accomplish the same thing on any LLM, although the results will obviously differ.

Here are some examples of tasks that ChatGPT can help you with, should you give it the prompt and examples to work from:

- **Headline and Summary Generation**: You can ask ChatGPT to help craft engaging LinkedIn headlines and summaries based on your professional background and goals. This works great when you have samples from "role models" that you would like to emulate.
- **Content Creation**: ChatGPT can help draft LinkedIn posts, articles, and even personalized connection requests. You can input a few key points regarding what you would like to talk about, and ChatGPT can generate a polished piece of content. The more it understands your voice, the better the results.
- **Message Personalization**: ChatGPT can help tailor messages for connecting with new contacts, responding to

inquiries, or nurturing relationships. The more context you provide, the higher the chance you have of receiving suggestions for personalized messages that resonate with the recipient.

- **Engagement Strategies**: ChatGPT can suggest engagement tactics, such as how to comment on a post in a way that adds value or how to start a meaningful conversation with a prospect.
- **Profile Optimization Tips**: You can ask ChatGPT for advice on optimizing different sections of your LinkedIn profile, such as which keywords to use or how to best present your professional experience.

As hinted at above, in order to get the best results from ChatGPT, you will need to be as specific as possible with your prompts, provide as much context as possible (I recommend you include actual samples of work that you would like to emulate to help "educate" ChatGPT and provide it training data), and understand that you will more often than not need to iterate on suggestions that come from ChatGPT to fine-tune its output.

How to Best Collaborate with ChatGPT

I often get asked what specific "prompts" I recommend for LinkedIn. To be honest, I don't believe in feeding generic prompts to ChatGPT. Instead, whenever I have a need, I have a natural conversation with ChatGPT, providing it as much information as possible but also asking it if it has any further questions for me to help it provide its best answer. Let me share a recent conversation I had to give you ideas on how to best leverage ChatGPT, not just for LinkedIn but also for any professional or personal pursuit you might have:

ME: [Note: I always begin with the role that I want ChatGPT to play and any context regarding my request, as you can see in this example.] You are an expert in creating content that gets a lot of user engagement on LinkedIn and goes viral. This means you both deeply understand the LinkedIn algorithm and are an excellent copywriter who can adapt stories and data to the formats that go viral on LinkedIn. Are you ready for my question?

CHATGPT: Absolutely! I'm ready to help you craft engaging LinkedIn content that resonates deeply, aligns with the algorithm, and has real viral potential. What's your question?

ME: I have a question about my LinkedIn professional headline. Can you help me with that as well?

CHATGPT: Definitely! Your LinkedIn professional headline is a critical part of your profile—it acts as your digital elevator pitch, setting the tone for every interaction you have on the platform.

Tell me more about what your current headline is, what you want it to accomplish (e.g., attract speaking opportunities, clients, or readers), and what specific positioning or keywords you'd like to emphasize. I'd be happy to provide you with strategic suggestions and refinements to help you stand out clearly and compellingly.

ME: So this is my current one:

Helping SMBs Scale w/ Digital Marketing | Fractional CMO | Global Speaker | 6X Author [Digital Threads, Maximizing LinkedIn for Business Growth, Age of Influence] | University Educator | Fluent in Japanese and Mandarin

I am thinking about simplifying it with my USP: I help businesses DIY their digital marketing to save money and grow their business smartly.

I also like one of my peers, who has this headline:

Marketing Creative + Behavioral Science | Award-Winning Author | International Keynote Speaker | Chief Creative Officer

Based on the above, and knowing what you know about me and who I serve and how I serve them, can you recommend a few LinkedIn professional headlines that I can use?

CHATGPT: Absolutely—I love that you're looking to simplify your LinkedIn headline by clearly communicating your unique value proposition. The goal here is clarity, relevance, and capturing attention quickly, aligning closely with your personal brand and audience.

Here are a few strategic headline options that leverage your USP while maintaining credibility and authority:

Option 1 (Clear and Direct USP)

I Help Businesses DIY Digital Marketing to Save Money and Grow Smarter | Fractional CMO | Global Speaker | Best-Selling Author

Option 2 (Focused on Impact and Practicality)

Teaching Entrepreneurs & SMBs to Grow Smart by Doing Their Own Digital Marketing | Award-Winning Author & Global Speaker

Option 3 (Emphasizing Your Expertise and Teaching Role)

Digital Marketing Educator Empowering SMBs & Entrepreneurs to Scale Smartly | Fractional CMO | Global Keynote Speaker | 6X Author

Option 4 (Concise & Authoritative)

DIY Digital Marketing Growth for SMBs | Fractional CMO | Best-Selling Author | International Speaker

Option 5 (Leveraging Credibility and Personality)

Guiding Businesses to Master DIY Digital Marketing and Scale Smart | Global Speaker | Author of Digital Threads & Maximizing LinkedIn

Each of these maintains your authority and expertise while emphasizing your key differentiator: enabling SMBs to "do-it-yourself," save money, and scale smartly. They're concise enough to be quickly readable, keyword-rich for LinkedIn SEO, and persuasive enough to instantly communicate your value.

Do any of these resonate most strongly, or would you like to refine further?

I hope that the above example will show you how to best collaborate with ChatGPT for any output that you want to get out of it. Remember, a combination of 1) the more training data, both from your own content and from relevant industry peers, that you provide it, as well as 2) the more conversations you have with ChatGPT over time, will allow the LLM to better understand your voice, tone, vocabulary usage, professional skills, hobbies, etc. The result will be responses that, over time, will sound more natural, as if you had written them, and less generic, which sound like they were literally AI-generated.

While powerful AI tools like ChatGPT can undoubtedly help with a boost in creativity, enhanced personalization, and sheer speed and efficiency, it is critically important that you review and personalize all its suggestions to ensure they align with your unique voice and brand. Sounding like AI-generated content instead of a human will only lessen your engagement on LinkedIn and make it harder to achieve the results you are looking for in reading this book!

Introducing the ASKNEAL™ Framework for Prompting ChatGPT

To help you consistently get the best results from ChatGPT, I've developed a simple, memorable framework I call **ASKNEAL™**. This step-by-step approach ensures you guide the tool in a way that reflects your intent, voice, and vision—every time. Whether you're brainstorming content, writing copy, or solving a problem, **ASKNEAL** will help you work smarter with AI.

Here's how it works:

A – Assign ChatGPT a Role: Tell ChatGPT whether you need a writer, strategist, editor, analyst, coach, or prompt engineer. This helps narrow the model's vast knowledge into a specific mode of operation.

S – State Your Objective: What do you want? Do you need a headline? Or perhaps a 500-word blog post? Maybe you need a list of 10 content ideas. Explicit requests lead to improved outputs.

K – Kickstart Context: Give ChatGPT the background: Who is your audience? What's the tone? What's the goal of the piece? Context builds relevance.

N – Name Your Inspiration: If you've written something before, or have seen examples that capture the style you want, share them. The more reference points you provide, the closer ChatGPT can get to what you're looking for.

E – Expand Upon the Idea: Share any additional thoughts, constraints, background info, or context that didn't fit earlier. This step helps ensure ChatGPT sees the full picture before creating its output.

A – Ask for Clarification: Before you submit your prompt—or after the first output—ask ChatGPT what it might need to know to do a better job. Sometimes the smartest prompts are the ones you didn't think to ask.

L – Lead the Iteration: Once you have a draft, improve it through collaboration. Don't settle for the first output. Push for clarity, tone, structure, or voice until it feels right.

This framework has powered the way I collaborate with ChatGPT across my entire digital marketing operation. It's how I write faster, think bigger, and stay on-brand. And now it's yours to use too.

So the next time you're sitting in front of a blinking cursor, wondering what to say—just remember to **ASKNEAL**™.

ASKNEAL™ FRAMEWORK FOR COLLABORATING WITH CHATGPT

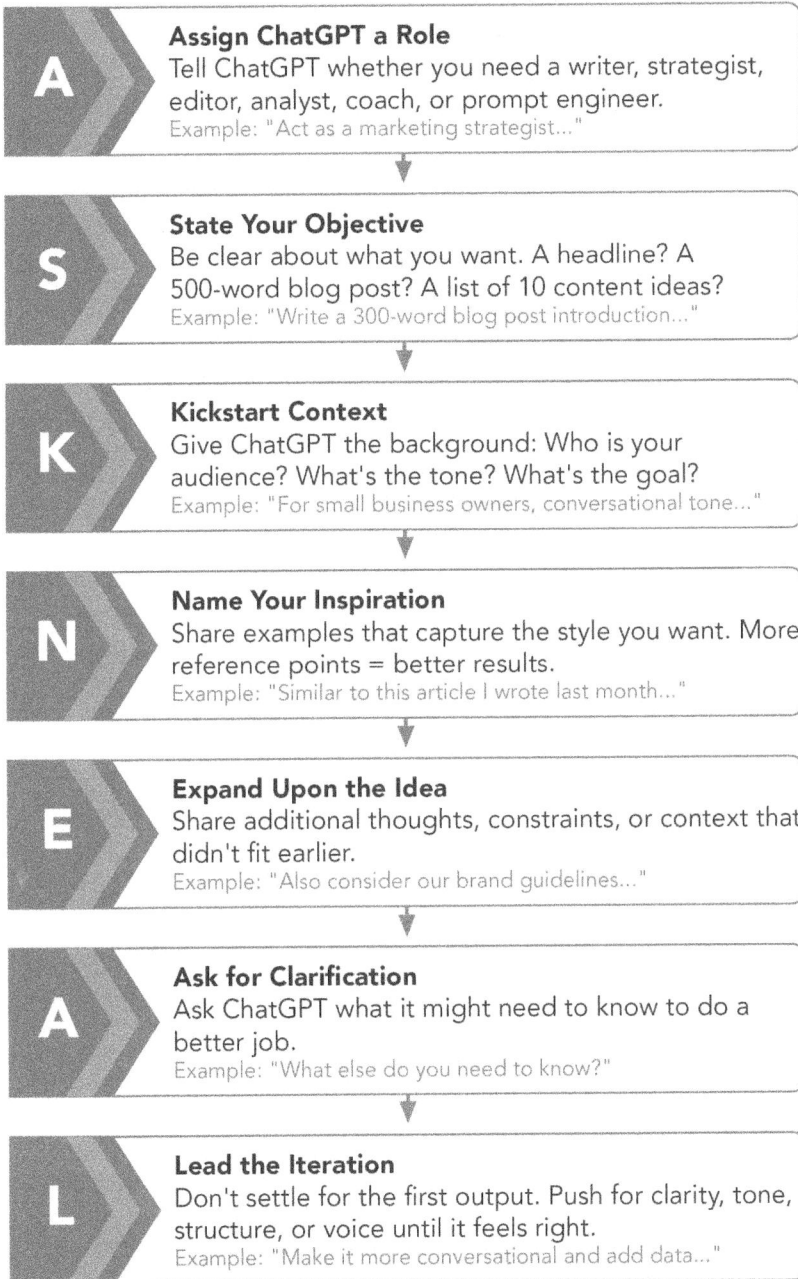

A

Assign ChatGPT a Role
Tell ChatGPT whether you need a writer, strategist, editor, analyst, coach, or prompt engineer.
Example: "Act as a marketing strategist..."

S

State Your Objective
Be clear about what you want. A headline? A 500-word blog post? A list of 10 content ideas?
Example: "Write a 300-word blog post introduction..."

K

Kickstart Context
Give ChatGPT the background: Who is your audience? What's the tone? What's the goal?
Example: "For small business owners, conversational tone..."

N

Name Your Inspiration
Share examples that capture the style you want. More reference points = better results.
Example: "Similar to this article I wrote last month..."

E

Expand Upon the Idea
Share additional thoughts, constraints, or context that didn't fit earlier.
Example: "Also consider our brand guidelines..."

A

Ask for Clarification
Ask ChatGPT what it might need to know to do a better job.
Example: "What else do you need to know?"

L

Lead the Iteration
Don't settle for the first output. Push for clarity, tone, structure, or voice until it feels right.
Example: "Make it more conversational and add data..."

Let's now move on to some task-specific AI tools I recommend you check out for specific purposes.

Using AI to Create Professional Headshots

As I discussed in the earlier chapter on profile photos, your LinkedIn headshot is a cornerstone of your personal brand—it's the first impression most people get when they land on your profile. If hiring a professional photographer isn't practical right now, dedicated AI tools can help you create or enhance a headshot that looks polished, professional, and aligned with your brand.

AI LinkedIn headshot tools start with a base photo you provide and use advanced machine learning to improve image quality, adjust backgrounds, and even change clothing to suit your industry. Many can subtly remove blemishes or distractions while keeping the image authentic—helping you project professionalism without looking overly edited.

The benefits go beyond cost savings. AI tools allow you to create high-quality headshots from home, experiment with multiple styles, and quickly refresh your photo whenever you update your look. This flexibility makes them ideal for keeping your profile current without the time and expense of booking a shoot.

I have a dedicated blog post reviewing 11 such tools, but here are five I recommend:[1]

- Aragon.ai (https://nealschaffer.com/aragon)
- HeadshotPro (https://nealschaffer.com/headshotpro)
- ProPhotos (https://nealschaffer.com/prophotos)
- Dreamwave (https://nealschaffer.com/dreamwave)
- Secta (https://nealschaffer.com/secta)

Most importantly, AI tools allow you to create high-quality headshots from the comfort of your home without relying on a professional photographer. That way, not only will you save money, but you'll also save a lot of time.

Curious what AI-generated headshots can look like? Below, you'll see examples from my session using Aragon.ai (and approved by my wife!).

MY AI HEADSHOT SAMPLES

Designing Branded LinkedIn Cover Images with AI

As mentioned earlier in Chapter 3, a good LinkedIn cover image should reinforce your personal or company brand and make your profile stand out. While your company might provide you with one to use, or you can upload a stock photo of a symbolic location or scenery, personal branding is all about controlling the narrative of you. For that reason, consider creating your own custom banner to put on display at the top of your LinkedIn profile so that you can incorporate the logos, taglines, and relevant visuals to communicate your brand effectively.

Before using AI, you have three other options if you want to create your own custom banner:

1. Use a graphics tool that includes LinkedIn banner templates that you can easily customize, such as **Adobe Express** (https://express.adobe.com/).
2. Work with one of the thousand people who can create a custom LinkedIn banner for you for as little as $5 on **Fiverr** (https://nealschaffer.com/fiverr).
3. **aiCarousels** (https://aicarousels.com/free-tools/linkedin-banner-maker-free) is a free tool that allows you to customize easily and then download a LinkedIn banner for the price of sharing their tool in a LinkedIn status update.

I recommend the following tools as additional AI LinkedIn cover image-generators:

- **Simplified** (https://simplified.com/create/linkedin-banners?fpr=neal65)
- **Appypie** (https://appypie.com/design/linkedin-banner/maker)
- **Designs.ai** (https://designs.ai/design-types/linkedin-banners)
- **Sivi** (https://sivi.ai/usecases/linkedin-profile-banner-generator)

- **Recraft** (https://recraft.ai/generate/linkedin-banners)

Crafting Engaging LinkedIn Headlines with AI

Your headline is one of the most visible and important parts of a LinkedIn profile. While you can certainly and easily create your own maximum 220-character version, AI can provide a sound foundation, which you can then further personalize to reflect your unique value proposition. This was on display in the sample ChatGPT conversation that I provided earlier in this chapter.

While third-party AI tools exist for this purpose, I would simply use ChatGPT as in my example, leveraging the **ASKNEAL**™ framework. To get the best results, make sure you are clear about what you want to promote in your headline and give one, if not multiple, samples from your peers that represent headlines you think are effective.

Enhancing Your LinkedIn Summary with AI Insights

One of the most powerful parts of your LinkedIn profile in terms of your personal branding is your LinkedIn summary. As you know, a well-crafted summary can attract the right connections and opportunities. AI can provide valuable input to enhance your summary while still allowing for your own personal touch.

Similar to my example of creating a LinkedIn headline with ChatGPT using the **ASKNEAL**™ framework, you can use the same process to create your summary.

Expect some back and forth when you get your first response, but following the framework will yield the results you are looking for based on your tone, voice, and training data.

Generating Engaging LinkedIn Content with ChatGPT

Consistent content creation is key to maintaining visibility on LinkedIn. If you plan on joining my challenge in regularly publishing status updates on LinkedIn to engage with your network, become more discoverable, and increase your thought leadership, start your journey on the hamster wheel of content that many marketers like me dread. Crafting engaging captions for your status updates can be time-consuming, but AI can help generate creative and relevant text quickly.

While I only recommend ChatGPT for your headline or summary, several LinkedIn-specific AI content generation tools have emerged that you might want to look into. But before that, I would begin experimenting with ChatGPT using my **ASKNEAL™** framework.

Here, the training data will be key to delivering the best results. If you have already published content on LinkedIn before, go through your analytics and look for the best-performing posts you can feed ChatGPT.

Remember the content search strategy I introduced in Chapter 6 for engaging with others? That same technique becomes invaluable in finding training data for AI content creation. You can search LinkedIn for specific keywords or phrases that you want to be known for, then filter the results by "Posts" to see what's currently performing well in those topic areas.

Simply type your target keyword or phrase into LinkedIn's search bar, filter by "Posts," and scroll through to find samples that are getting strong engagement (look for double-digit likes, comments, and shares). This gives you real-world examples of content that's resonating with LinkedIn's audience right now—perfect training data for ChatGPT to model your own content after. Below is a screenshot of what this looks like. You can even search for posts by specific LinkedIn users whose style you admire, as I've done below!

SAMPLE LINKEDIN POST SEARCH

Generating Engaging LinkedIn Content with Third-Party AI Tools

If you've read this far, you've likely already bought into the idea that LinkedIn is a powerful content platform and that AI can play a role in making your content strategy more efficient and impactful.

So far, I have introduced how you can use ChatGPT for everything from optimizing your profile to generating ideas for what to post. But what if I told you that there are other tools, specifically designed for LinkedIn, that can help you generate potentially higher-performing content in less time?

Let me explain.

When we think of content optimization, we often think about SEO. Before publishing a blog post, we check keyword trends, analyze top-ranking pages, and structure our content to match what we believe Google wants. That data-driven approach separates random bloggers from those who consistently generate traffic.

And yet, many professionals still treat LinkedIn content like a shot in the dark.

They post updates based on gut feeling, recycle content from other platforms, or only promote their own services—without thinking about how the LinkedIn algorithm works or what content performs well.

I have already educated you on the algorithm and its basic workings, together with the different content format types. The truth is, though, if you think about it, LinkedIn has an algorithm just like Google. And just like with SEO, there are now tools that analyze what works, track engagement trends, and help you structure your posts for maximum visibility.

That's why I've changed my stance on using third-party tools beyond ChatGPT for LinkedIn.

In the past, I was hesitant to recommend too many third-party AI writing tools. Many developers built them for general-purpose use; therefore, they lack the focus needed to truly optimize content for any one platform. That's why I suggested sticking with ChatGPT—at least you can train it to reflect your voice.

But LinkedIn-specific tools are different.

They're not just content generators. They act more like SEO tools, but for LinkedIn.

These platforms analyze LinkedIn's most successful posts across industries. They identify patterns, track formats, and surface hooks, tones, and structures that are resonating with users—right now.

Instead of starting with a blank page, you're starting with informed inspiration. And that changes everything.

Here's what makes these tools unique compared to generic AI apps:

- They track high-performing LinkedIn posts across industries and creators.
- They analyze engagement metrics like reactions, comments, and shares.
- They identify what types of posts (text, carousels, commentary, visuals) get the most visibility.
- They provide post templates and topic suggestions based on real data.
- Some even integrate your past content to tailor suggestions to your brand voice.

Think of them as a personal LinkedIn strategist, one that's working 24/7 to surface proven content strategies for your niche.

Just like SEO tools help you understand what's working on Google, these tools help you understand what's working on LinkedIn. And that shift from random posting to data-driven strategy is what can make all the difference.

While several tools exist, one of the most comprehensive I've used is Taplio. Here's an overview of what it can do:

- **Generated for You**: AI-generated text posts based on your industry and writing preferences—updated daily.
- **Post Generator**: Create custom posts by entering your bio, audience, and topic, along with the goal of the post (inspirational, actionable, or promotional).
- **Carousel Generator**: Enter a blog URL, YouTube link, or prompt and generate an AI-driven carousel with editable visuals.
- **Repurpose Content**: Quickly turn your blog posts or videos into native LinkedIn content.

- **Viral Post Inspiration**: See what posts are already performing well on LinkedIn—and adapt them into your own voice and experience.
- **Search Mode**: Use keywords to manually browse high-performing posts and generate similar ones.
- **Industry News Commentary**: Choose from curated articles and have AI generate status updates expressing agreement or disagreement—ready for your input.

I have easily created a LinkedIn carousel post in Taplio by repurposing one of my blog posts. Below is a screenshot of the user interface to give you a feel for how easy it is to create these:

GENERATING A LINKEDIN CAROUSEL IN TAPLIO

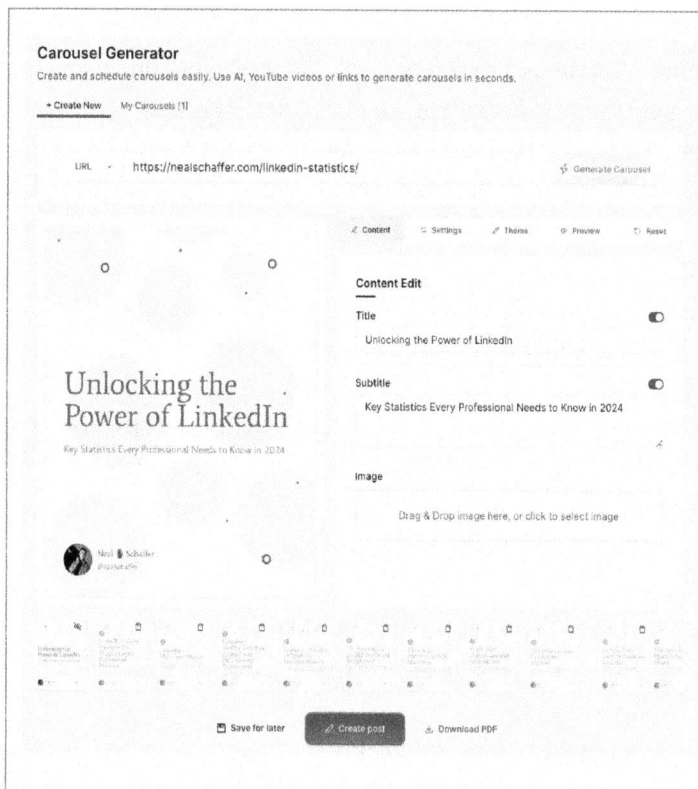

Taplio is not officially integrated with LinkedIn's API, so it works with publicly available content in creative ways. Think of it like hiring an assistant who reads the entire LinkedIn newsfeed daily and tells you what's working.

Taplio is one of many tools that have emerged, and that I have tried out and spoken to the founders of. Here is a shortlist of the tools that I recommend you check out:

- **Taplio** (https://nealschaffer.com/taplio)
- **ContentIn** (https://nealschaffer.com/contentin)
- **Saywhat** (https://nealschaffer.com/saywhat)

A Word of Caution: You Still Need to Be Human

Let me be clear: I'm not advocating that you outsource your entire content strategy to a tool.

Just like with ChatGPT, the quality of the output depends on how you use it. AI can give you a sound starting point, but the final version must reflect your voice, tone, experience, and authenticity. I never recommend copy-pasting anything that AI gives you. Always revise. Always personalize.

If you've read this book carefully, you know that trust and credibility matter on LinkedIn. That's why your audience needs to hear you in every word, even if AI helped write the first draft.

I encourage you to try one of these tools and use it regularly for a few weeks. Compare your content's performance to what you were doing before. Measure profile views, connection requests, comments, and reach. Treat LinkedIn content the way you'd treat SEO content—with a mindset of testing, measuring, and optimizing.

You'll soon see patterns.

You'll understand what kinds of posts draw people in.

You'll wonder less about what to write and spend more time engaging with people who are finally seeing your content.

That's the goal: not just to create content—but to create content that works.

Chapter 11
Using a Personal CRM to Stay Organized on LinkedIn

Most people think success on social media is all about getting more views, more clicks, more followers. But I want to challenge that mindset because the real gold is in your inbox.

If you've ever looked back and realized you lost touch with a potential client or forgot to follow up with someone who was genuinely interested in working together, you're not alone. And the culprit isn't a lack of content or charisma—it's simply the absence of a system.

After publishing the first version of this book last year, I realized that something critical was missing, which might hold back your success in using LinkedIn: systems for organizing and following up.

Let me walk you through what changed for me and why this could be the single most valuable shift you can make in how you use LinkedIn.

The Moment I Knew I Was Dropping the Ball

While revising this book, I had what I call a "DM epiphany." I was knee-deep in content planning and reflecting on past collaborations, and I started scrolling back through my LinkedIn messages. The volume of missed conversations (people I *meant* to follow up with but never did) was staggering.

It wasn't just prospects. It was podcasters I never circled back to. People I'd met at conferences. Book reviewers. Collaborators. Friends. All buried under hundreds of newer threads.

And that's when I realized: I had an inbox problem.

More importantly, I had a system problem. I was relying on social inboxes, like LinkedIn Messaging and Instagram DMs, which weren't built for organization. I couldn't tag or sort people. I couldn't set reminders. I couldn't easily follow up.

That's when I knew: If I wanted to fully tap into the relationships I'd worked so hard to build, I needed a personal CRM.

What Is a Personal CRM, and Why You Need One

You might think: *Neal, I'm not in sales. Why would I need a CRM?*

That's exactly the problem.

I have tried using spreadsheets and notes applications to manage various correspondences and dates regarding relationships, but ended up with a scattered collection of data that requires putting in all the work to manage.

There is a better solution.

Enter the personal CRM—or PRM, personal relationship manager. This is not solely for those in sales. It's for creators, consultants, entrepreneurs, marketers, and really any professional who builds relationships online. Closing deals is not what this is about. It's about not dropping the ball with the people who already know, like, and trust you.

A true personal CRM helps you:

- Tag and categorize your connections
- Set reminders to follow up
- Track past conversations across channels
- Identify who hasn't responded—and who to try contacting again

- Reignite cold conversations with context

In short, it's how you stop treating LinkedIn like a billboard and start treating it like the relationship hub it is.

From Inbox Chaos to Inbox Clarity: My Journey with Kondo

I've used CRMs in the past. In fact, one of the first I used was Goldmine, back in my B2B sales days. That was decades ago, before anyone invented the "cloud"—and now many CRMs exist, with Salesforce being the most famous.

But it wasn't until recently that I discovered Kondo (https://nealschaffer.com/kondo)—a tool designed specifically to turn your LinkedIn inbox into something usable. It is not a CRM, but it shares some features and has become an invaluable tool for organizing my network.

While my intention in writing this book is to give you as evergreen advice as possible (and thus, I hate to overly rely on one tool), this is a one-of-a-kind tool that I have built a process around, and I think you will find it invaluable. As you become more active on LinkedIn after following my advice, your network, as well as your conversations with LinkedIn users in your network, will only increase over time, and thus, you, too, will find value in this tool.

Kondo pulls your LinkedIn messages into a clean, Gmail-like interface. Here is a screenshot to help you re-imagine what your LinkedIn Inbox *could* look like:

YOUR LINKEDIN INBOX REIMAGINED IN KONDO

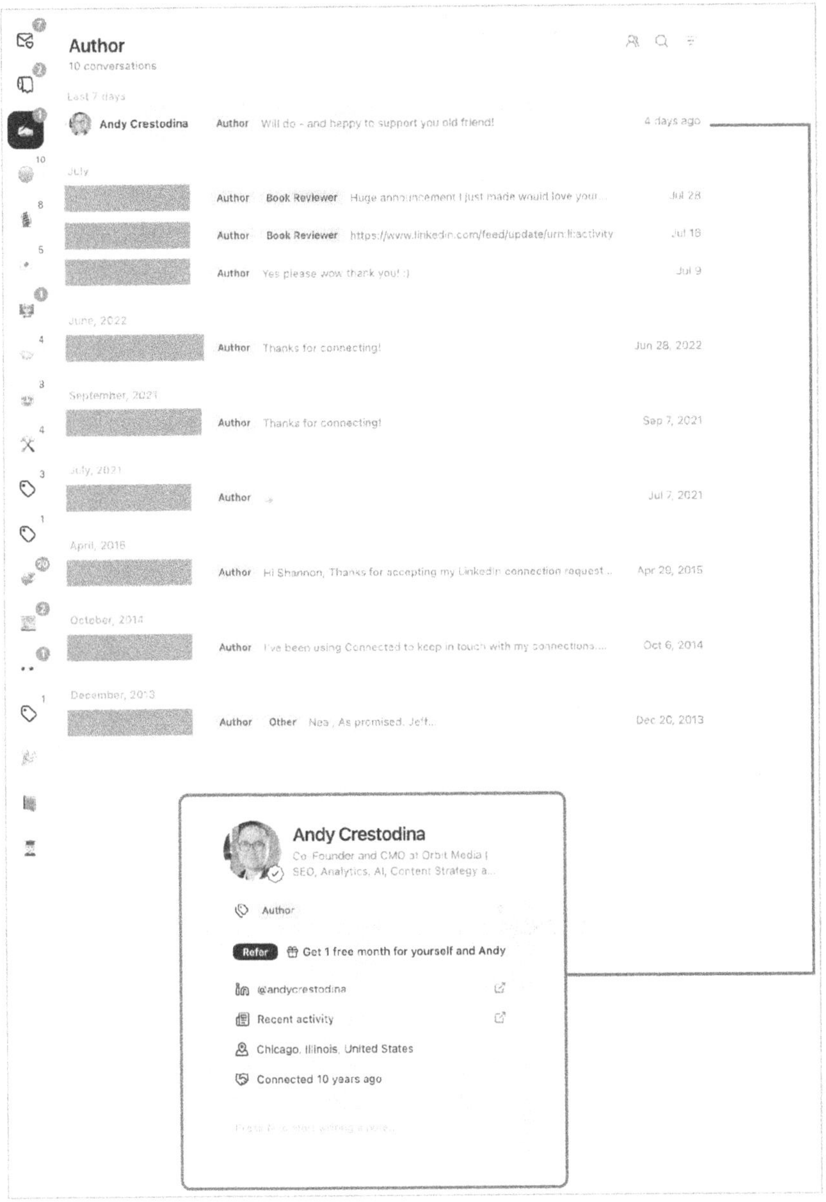

What you see on the left-hand side are tags with which I organize my connections. The current view is of the Authors tag, so when I receive a message from an author or I have a reason to reach out to other authors, I can easily do so.

The screenshot only hints at what is possible. Kondo allows you to:

- Tag people by interest, niche, or opportunity type (think: referral partners, prospects, college alumni, local network, recruiters)
- Set reminders to follow up, after which the message will appear at the top of your inbox again (no more "meant to get back to you!")
- Use templates and snippets to respond quickly and consistently
- Track who replied and who didn't

It's like bringing Inbox Zero into your social media life. And for someone like me, who's always chasing clarity in the chaos? Game-changer.

Since adopting Kondo, I've been going through old, neglected messages and processing a month's worth of LinkedIn messages per day. Every day, I'm finding new leads, revisiting old opportunities, and staying connected in ways I hadn't before.

Beyond LinkedIn: Creating a True Personal CRM System

While Kondo helps me manage my LinkedIn inbox, the bigger opportunity is building a true personal CRM system across *all* channels. Because your important contacts don't just live on LinkedIn.

You also have:

- Gmail threads with collaborators
- Calendar invites with customers and prospects
- Newsletter subscriber lists
- Webinar attendees

- Outreach lists
- Facebook messages
- Instagram DMs
- Twitter/X replies

And if you're like most people, all those conversations live in silos: untagged, untracked, and unorganized.

That's why the next step is finding a personal CRM that lets you centralize all of that. Once again, it is not necessarily about sales and pipeline management but about professional networking and people management. Kondo will help you organize your contacts into logical groups and keep in better touch on LinkedIn. A personal CRM will now allow you to extend this to all your channels.

For personal CRMs, several options are in the market, so I encourage you to try a few to find the best one for your specific needs. Here are a few I've been testing:

- **Nimble (https://nimble.com/)**: Jon Ferrara, a pioneer in the space and founder of the previously mentioned Goldmine, created one of the most established "social CRMs." It has solid Gmail, social integrations, and even email sequences now. A great all-around tool if you like robust functionality.
- **Breakcold (https://breakcold.com/)**: Another strong option with a Chrome extension and social integrations. Similar to Nimble, Breakcold stands out for showing social activity feeds inside the CRM—great for building rapport.
- **Folk (https://folk.app/)**: A newer CRM that stands out for its simplicity and Chrome extension. You can add people from LinkedIn or the web, organize contacts, and create email campaigns easily. It's lightweight and intuitive—great for creators and solopreneurs.
- **Clay (https://clay.earth/)**: One of the most innovative CRMs I've seen. It's built specifically for relationship management, not sales. It tells you when people change jobs, nudges you to reconnect, and integrates across

platforms. The only drawback: Email functionality is still limited.

- **Relatable (https://try.relatable.one/)**: Another truly personal CRM that is like Clay in some aspects but also has some gamification features and follow-up by tag settings that make it easier for you to manage your connections. This tool is the newest on the list and was developed by the same entrepreneur who developed Contactually, an innovative CRM bought out by the real estate company Compass.

Each of these has strengths and weaknesses, and no tool is perfect. The key is to pick one that fits your workflow and helps you create a habit around relationship management.

How to Build Your Personal CRM System

You don't need to overhaul your tech stack overnight. Start small. Here's the exact playbook I recommend:

1. **Audit Your Conversations**. Where are most of your meaningful conversations happening—LinkedIn? Email? Instagram DMs? Choose one place to start.
2. **Pick One Tool**. Start with Kondo for LinkedIn or one of the CRMs above for broader use. Don't overthink it; just start organizing.
3. **Sync or Import Your Contacts**. This is where you actually add your contacts to the CRM database. If you use Kondo, you can sync your tags (see below) with your CRM to add your network selectively as you organize. All the other CRMs have integrations with LinkedIn, normally through a Chrome extension, that allow you to do the same. The other option is to export your LinkedIn connections and then import them into your CRM. You can do that on LinkedIn by going to

Settings & Privacy – Data privacy – Get a copy of your data, and then choose the option that begins with "Download larger data archive, including connections…" Note that it can take 24 hours to download this from LinkedIn.

4. **Tag and Group Your Contacts.** If you have already started tagging in Kondo, it might be too late, but if you want to import your contacts and then tag them in your CRM, it's best to start with a logical grouping of your network. This is where everyone will categorize their connections differently, but try to think holistically about your tags based on relationships you have with your network, not just sales:

   - People I Want to Get to Know Better
   - Old Colleagues
   - Past Clients
   - Prospects
   - Influencers
   - Thought Leaders
   - Partners
   - Journalists
   - Superfans
   - Alumni
   - Friends
   - Local Connections

5. **Set Weekly Follow-Up Time.** The hard part is in the setup of the CRM. Once you have your contacts in your database of choice, block off 15 minutes a day or one hour a week to organize your tags and follow up with people you've lost touch with. Treat it like a meeting with your future opportunities.

6. **Reignite Old Threads.** Start with people you haven't spoken to in three to six months or even longer. A simple personal message is all it takes to reopen a conversation.

7. **Track Replies and Stay Consistent.** If someone doesn't

reply, set a reminder and try again in a few weeks. The best relationships often need a second nudge.

The Real ROI of a Personal CRM

You won't see the ROI of this immediately. It won't show up in your LinkedIn analytics. It won't go viral. You won't get dopamine hits from likes and comments.

But what *will* you get?

- More opportunities
- More referrals
- Stronger relationships
- More closed loops

In a world where social media reach is shrinking and search algorithms are unpredictable, your best leads are the people you already know. You simply need to stay in better touch.

Organizing your relationships on LinkedIn and regularly following up is the missing link that turns all your effort into sustained results.

Think about it: you spend hours crafting content, building your brand, growing your network…and then let it all slide through the cracks if you don't follow up.

Let's change that.

You don't need a team or a complicated sales pipeline. You just need a system—and the commitment to show up.

Because your next big opportunity? It's probably already in your inbox.

Having a personal CRM system is powerful, but only if you use it consistently. Next, let's create a daily LinkedIn routine that ensures you're maximizing every tool and strategy we've covered.

Chapter 12
Creating a LinkedIn Playbook: Building a Daily Routine for Success

I already hinted at developing a playbook to help you keep in better touch with your growing network in Chapter 6 on engaging on LinkedIn. I want to devote this chapter to applying that same concept to helping you better organize and implement your daily activity on LinkedIn.

Even the most organized and confident among us need a playbook to remind us of what we should do daily and keep our activities on track to ensure we are using our time wisely. This becomes the set plan for efficiently maximizing your presence on LinkedIn. For a playbook to be effective, you'll want to stick with it as much as possible, but you should also optimize it over time as you find some actions result in more business or ROI than others.

I used to have a chapter on LinkedIn automation tools in this guide, but I removed it because, among other reasons, those tools simply replicate a type of playbook that I am going to teach you how to create here. I have heard of way too many people who have gotten kicked off or put in "LinkedIn jail" to recommend you take on this risk, and I think you will be more successful on LinkedIn by focusing on developing your own relationships organically through engagement and the publishing of your own content.

Playbooks have several elements, but your LinkedIn playbook should focus on the following five elements:

Curating Strategic Connections

Your LinkedIn network becomes an invaluable asset over time, so why not try to develop it on a regular basis? Ideally, you should be able to add a few new connections to your network regularly if you have an outgoing role or meet people at events. As I said earlier in this book, it's important to not cold-invite people to be your connections. Therefore, when starting out, you'll probably only be inviting people you already know from other places before branching out.

At the same time, you'll want to cultivate future connections. As you meet new people offline and online, make sure you follow up with a LinkedIn connection request. And if you are searching for prospects or other LinkedIn users who might help you meet your professional objectives and notice you share many mutual connections, don't be afraid to consider sending them an invitation to connect.

Maximizing Engagement Impact

Make it a policy to engage for a few minutes or with a certain number of posts on a regular basis and stick with it. By engaging regularly, you'll be making yourself more recognizable within your network and, over time, to your network's connections. This should help increase the size of your network, boost engagement with your content, and deepen relationships with your network and those you aim to engage with.

You could divide this up to, say, engage with five posts from your own network that you see in your newsfeed as well as five posts from five different prospects you follow and want to engage with. For maximum effectiveness, engage with content that is aligned with your professional brand and you truly resonate with, and consider leaving a thoughtful comment instead of a mere "like" for maximum impact.

Streamlining Your Publishing Strategy

Make sure that some kind of publishing happens regularly. Ideally, publish a status update at least once every week. People come to LinkedIn to keep track of professionals and their companies, so it's important to make sure your profile is a happening place. Over time, you'll learn the ideal publishing frequency for you and your company, but by publishing content you are "showing up" in the influential and potentially lucrative news feeds of your network (and should they engage with your content, your connection's network) and win their attention.

To facilitate the regular publishing of content, I recommend you create some sort of plan for what content you publish and how frequently and at what time you will publish it. LinkedIn gives you the ability to schedule status updates in the future, so take advantage of that and consider batch-scheduling your content on a weekly basis. I try to schedule my next week's batch of content every Friday.

I already gave you ideas on what content to publish in Chapter 9, so you could schedule out your content and publish five different types of content each weekday. Or you could pick a theme like resharing company page posts on Mondays, thought leadership type of opinion content on Tuesdays, the latest industry news on Wednesday, upcoming events you will attend on Thursdays, and more casual selfies on Fridays as an early start to the weekend.

There are two benefits in planning out your content for the future in this manner:

1. It makes it easier for you to create content knowing what content medium or subject you need to create content for.
2. It helps you analyze which content medium and subject gets the most engagement, which you can then lean into and prioritize for greater effectiveness.

All this advice about creating a content calendar or using scheduling tools is meant to help you maintain consistency in publishing, which is key to building a strong LinkedIn presence. Without them, your efforts and outcomes might be a bit more random.

Proactive Prospecting and Follow-Up

This one's mostly for salespeople and business development professionals. Without new sales prospects, our business would dry up fast. That's why it is important that we continually check in with people who might be interested in our products and services. Job hunters have a different perspective on this: The more hiring managers you come across in the course of a job search, the faster you're likely to get hired. Name recognition is just as important for jobs as it is for corporate sales. Don't lose sight of the people who can help you.

If you think of your LinkedIn activities as part of an engagement funnel, think of your prospects as being at the very top of that funnel. With that in mind, some suggested activities to do daily would include:

- looking for new people you can add to your relationship pipeline
- engaging with the content or profiles of a few people in your relationship pipeline
- asking for a warm introduction from one of your contacts to a potential prospect
- sending a connection request to a potential prospect (assuming you have lots of mutual connections who have warmed up to you)
- sending a direct message to a potential prospect to set up a meeting or invite to an event

While you want to execute efficiently on increasing connections, engaging, and the publishing aspects of your playbook, there is no limit to the amount of prospecting you should do!

Optimizing Your LinkedIn Routine

I believe that by committing to a playbook and writing out your daily plans, you can complete most tasks, outside of content creation, in as little as five minutes, and rarely over 15 minutes. If you spend more time and are still not seeing any results, it's time to dial your efforts back and see how to optimize them.

Here's the thing: Your LinkedIn playbook shouldn't be set in stone and instead should be a living document. You will find some of your efforts more impactful than others. That is why it is a best practice to review what's working periodically and adjust your routine as necessary.

LinkedIn provides you with some analytics that can help monitor the impact of your efforts, such as:

- how many impressions and engagement each published status update receives
- how many profile views you received
- how many times you appeared in LinkedIn searches
- growth in your number of followers

If you follow my advice, over time you should see growth in your profile views, a higher number of appearances in LinkedIn searches, and an increase in followers. Increased engagement on your status updates will depend on several factors that are harder to control, as the LinkedIn algorithm for the newsfeed is always in flux and prioritizing different things at different times.

Now that we've covered the different elements of a LinkedIn play-book, below is a visual representation of a sample LinkedIn playbook checklist for you to repurpose and use for your own particular needs.

YOUR SAMPLE LINKEDIN PLAYBOOK CHECKLIST

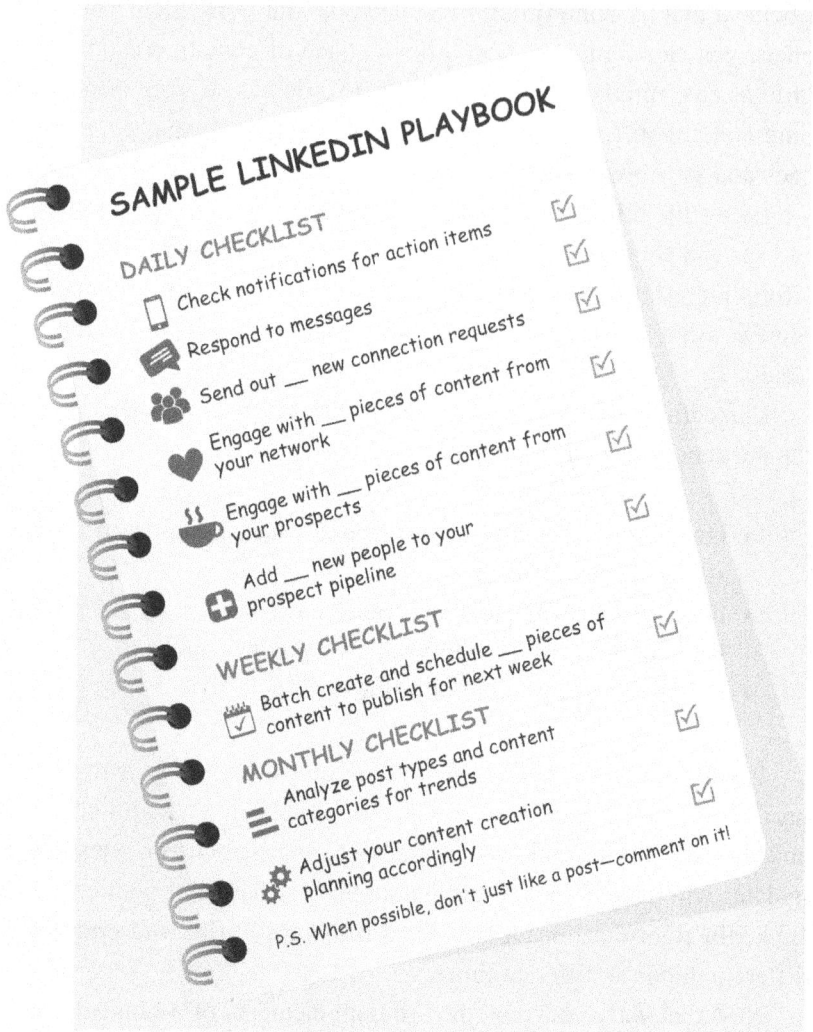

SAMPLE LINKEDIN PLAYBOOK

DAILY CHECKLIST

- ☑ Check notifications for action items
- ☑ Respond to messages
- ☑ Send out __ new connection requests
- ☑ Engage with __ pieces of content from your network
- ☑ Engage with __ pieces of content from your prospects
- ☑ Add __ new people to your prospect pipeline

WEEKLY CHECKLIST

- ☑ Batch create and schedule __ pieces of content to publish for next week

MONTHLY CHECKLIST

- ☑ Analyze post types and content categories for trends
- ☑ Adjust your content creation planning accordingly

P.S. When possible, don't just like a post—comment on it!

By following this playbook and consistently engaging with LinkedIn, you're taking proactive steps toward achieving your professional goals. Remember, success on LinkedIn, like in any aspect of business, comes from dedication, consistency, and a willingness to adapt and learn.

Chapter 13
LinkedIn Case Studies: Real-World Success Stories

W e've covered the strategies. We've walked through the framework. Now let's bring it all to life with actual stories of professionals and businesses who put this book's teachings into action and reaped measurable rewards on LinkedIn. These case studies aren't just examples; they're proof of what's possible when you apply these concepts consistently and intentionally. Think of them as playbooks in motion, each building upon the last.

How an Optimized LinkedIn Profile Landed a 7-Month Consulting Contract

Every success story begins with visibility.

That was Martin van Wunnik's (https://arsimaprojects.eu) first priority.[1] He didn't focus on lead magnets or fancy funnels. As an independent consultant based in Belgium, he knew he had to show up in searches before he could show up in someone's inbox.

So he optimized his LinkedIn profile like a high-intent landing page. He clarified his experience. He added keywords aligned with his experience and the projects he wanted, no matter how niche they might be. One of them, "consolidation," turned out to be the golden term.

That keyword matched the exact needs of a UK agency looking for help where Martin lived in Belgium. After a quick search, they viewed his profile, sent an outreach email, and just like that, they hired him.

The result? A seven-month consulting engagement that accounted for half his annual income that year.

Lesson: As you read in Chapter 3, search visibility is about alignment. Martin didn't have to chase opportunities. He positioned himself to be found. That's the power of a well-optimized LinkedIn profile.

How a Simple LinkedIn Status Update Sparked a Speaking Gig

If Martin's story proves the power of search, Sue Henry's (https://linkedin.com/in/suehenrytalks/) proves the magic of serendipity.

Sue, a social media educator, wasn't creating a buzz on LinkedIn—she was just sharing her work and clientele in a non-promotional way.[2] Then she posted an update like, "Just completed a proposal for a nonprofit that will help them increase online donations."

That single post set off a chain reaction.

An old contact (someone who'd attended one of her earlier classes) saw the post and referred her to a regional conference organizer. That organizer, intrigued, sat in on a future workshop without Sue's knowledge. Then came the message, the phone call, and eventually, the booking.

The reward? A speaking engagement that also led to course sales and new consulting opportunities, resulting in $1,200 of additional business generated from a single status update.

Lesson: In Chapter 9, I talked about the overlooked power of status updates. Sue's story shows that even short-form, textual content can drive real outcomes if it's framed with intent and shared consistently.

Building a Pipeline of Clients Through Consistent, Value-First LinkedIn Engagement

While Sue sparked results from a single post, Irina Maltseva (https://linkedin.com/in/irinamaltseva/) built hers brick by brick.

A growth marketer focused on SEO and SaaS, Irina didn't start on LinkedIn to sell.[3] She started serving simply by sharing her experiences as a marketer. Her content was generous and full of the tools, frameworks, and case studies she used with clients every day. Twice a week, she shared wins and failures, not to impress, but to teach.

The result? By 2024, 80% of her clients came inbound via LinkedIn.

Her profile functioned like a high-converting funnel, optimized with testimonials, results, and clear contact options. But it was her consistency and honesty that closed the deals. She showed up in comment threads. She replied to DMs. Rather than a stage, she treated LinkedIn as a conversation.

Lesson: Chapters 3, 6, and 9 are all about this synergy: profile optimization + engagement consistency + content credibility. Irina's story is proof that when you commit to the long game, LinkedIn becomes your strongest and most cost-effective channel for high-quality lead generation.

Turning Honest LinkedIn Posts into a Co-Founder Partnership

What if your content didn't just attract clients but partners?

That's exactly what happened to Tim Hanson (https://linkedin.com/in/tihanson/).[4] A content strategist by trade, Tim used LinkedIn like a journal. He documented what worked, what didn't, and what he wished more marketers talked about in his fields of expertise: SEO and content marketing.

Then came the DM that changed everything.

A reader-turned-client had been quietly following his posts. She was building an AI writing tool. His approach to content aligned perfectly with her product vision. They met. They clicked. Six months later, Penfriend was born—with Tim as co-founder.

He didn't post for fame. He posted for clarity. That clarity attracted someone who wasn't just interested in his ideas. They wanted to build something with him.

Tim's advice? "Make what YOU would want to read."

Lesson: Trust is the true currency of LinkedIn. When you consistently share your point of view, you magnetize the right people, sometimes not just for sales but for something far more meaningful.

Visibility That Led to a VP Role and a New Business

Tim's story showed the power of content in collaboration. Melanie Borden's (https://linkedin.com/in/melanieborden/) journey shows how it can reshape a career.[5]

She wasn't new to success. But until she started posting regularly, her accomplishments were mostly invisible to those outside her direct network. So she made a commitment: One post at a time, she'd start telling her story.

She didn't go viral. She went visible.

Her posts (honest, behind-the-scenes reflections on marketing and leadership) started gaining traction. Within a year, she'd landed a VP role in Martech. But the momentum didn't stop there. Questions started rolling in: "Can you help me build a brand like yours?"

Melanie turned her journey into a business model. She left the VP role and started her own firm, helping other executives step into the spotlight.

Lesson: You don't have to shout to stand out. When you speak directly to the right audience with consistent clarity, opportunity finds you, and sometimes it opens entirely new doors.

Replacing a Sales Team with Community-Built Demand on LinkedIn

Melanie's growth was steady. Elfried Samba's (https://linkedin.com/in/elfriedsamba/)? Explosive.

When he launched his community marketing agency, Butterfly Effect, Elfried made an unconventional decision: no sales team.[6] No cold outreach. No funnels. He would build everything through LinkedIn.

And that's exactly what he did.

In year one alone, the agency earned $2.6 million in inbound revenue. The secret? Daily storytelling. Team amplification. Humanized posts that sparked engagement not by being promotional but by being real.

In his own words, "LinkedIn wouldn't be a billboard. It would be the heartbeat of the business."

He and his team didn't just post. They participated. Comments, DMs, and threads were where they turned up. They didn't build a following. They built a movement.

Lesson: Community isn't a buzzword. It's a business model. Consistency and authenticity at scale on LinkedIn can replace traditional sales infrastructure. Elfried proved it.

Turning Sustainable Storytelling into an Enterprise Opportunity

And finally, Ben Read's (https://linkedin.com/in/benjaminrread/) story ties it all together.

Where Elfried built a company around community and trust, Ben used it to break into enterprise sales.[7] As the founder of Mercha, a sustainable merchandise company, Ben didn't sugarcoat the startup struggle. He showed the messy middle: 14 bamboo suppliers tested, partnerships rejected, processes rethought.

That honesty resonated.

One post about Mercha's sustainability journey caught the attention of a director at a major Australian retailer. That comment led to a coffee. The coffee led to a deal. The deal became one of their first enterprise clients.

No paid ads. No fancy funnel. Just candor and specificity in the right place at the right time.

Lesson: When your content reflects both what you believe and what you're solving, it becomes a shortcut to trust. Sharing your raw and authentic journey, flaws and all, is often your most powerful differentiator.

Will You Become My Next Case Study?

Every story you just read started with a decision: to show up. To be seen. To speak clearly. The tactics in this book are just the beginning. Your consistency, curiosity, and courage will do the rest.

So take what you've learned. Apply it. Refine it. And when your story unfolds (and I truly believe it will) I hope you'll share it with me.

Who knows?

You just might be the next case study in the next edition.

Connect with me and let me know how your LinkedIn journey develops: https://linkedin.com/in/nealschaffer.

Here's to your next chapter, on LinkedIn and beyond.

FREE LINKEDIN RESOURCES

◀◀◀ Accelerate Your Results ▶▶▶
with These Exclusive Downloads

LinkedIn QuickStart Checklist
30-day action plan with daily 15-minute tasks that build real momentum

Profile Optimization Checklist
Step-by-step guide to transform your profile into a client magnet

The ASKNEAL™ Framework
My exclusive system for getting authentic (not robotic) results from AI

Personal LinkedInPlaybookTemplate
Customizable daily routine that drives results in just 5-15 minutes

30-Day Content Ideas Calendar
Never wonder "what should I post?" again—includes templates and examples

Download All 5 FREE
Visit: nealschaffer.com/linkedinresources

Battle-tested strategies from professionals who've built successful businesses, landed dream jobs, and grown influential personal brands through LinkedIn.

Your breakthrough is one download away.

THANK YOU FOR READING MAXIMIZING LINKEDIN FOR BUSINESS GROWTH!

I appreciate any feedback and would love to hear
what you thought about Maximizing
LinkedIn for Business Growth
Your input is essential to help make this book
and make my future books
even better to serve more people.

Please take a minute now to leave a review on Amazon
letting me know what you thought of the book:

nealschaffer.com/maximizinglinkedinreview

I cannot thank you enough! If you used a non-recognizable name,
please send me a screenshot to neal@nealschaffer.com so that I can
personally thank you!

- Neal Schaffer

IF YOU LIKED
MAXIMIZING LINKEDIN FOR BUSINESS GROWTH,
YOU'LL LIKE MY OTHER BOOKS:

nealschaffer.com/digitalthreads

The small business and
entrepreneur playbook
for digital first marketing.

nealschaffer.com/ageofinfluence

The definitive guide to influencer marketing.

nealschaffer.com/maximizeyoursocial

The definitive guide to
creating and implementing a
social media marketing strategy.

nealschaffer.com/maximizinglinkedin

The definitive guide to using LinkedIn
for social selling, employee advocacy,
and social media marketing.

Visit **nealschaffer.com/books/**
for more information.

WORK WITH ME

I work with businesses in a variety of ways, from strategy creation to audit, implementation to training. Please find more information below and contact me below if I can be of any help to you or your organization.

GROUP COACHING

My Digital First Group Coaching Community includes four monthly Zoom calls, one quarterly 30-minute private coaching call, and a private Facebook Group.

PRIVATE COACHING

When you need one-on-one help. Provided in one-hour increments.

FRACTIONAL CMO

My signature marketing consulting service where I become your fractional CMO, and you leverage my expertise however you see fit. Flexible, cost-effective, and you retain all IP!

SPEAKING & TRAINING

Whether it is speaking at your event or hands-on training for your team, I can help.

nealschaffer.com/contact/

SUBSCRIBE

SUBSCRIBE TO MY NEWSLETTER

Every week I provide updates to my readers on the world of Digital Threads, including:

- **The latest digital marketing news**
- **Updates on search engine optimization**
- **Strategies for successful email marketing**
- **Trending topics in social media marketing including LinkedIn**
- **The newest AI technologies and tips for marketing**
- **My latest YouTube video, podcast episode, and blog posts**

In addition, this is the best way to find out about my new books, speaking events, and free educational webinars and other resources that I provide!

Subscribe here:
nealschaffer.com/newsletter/

Endnotes

1. LinkedIn Statistics: Understanding the Platform's Impact

1. LinkedIn Pressroom (n.d.). *Statistics*. https://news.linkedin.com/about-us#Statistics.
2. Dixon, S.J. (March 26, 2025a). Most used social networks 2025, by number of users. *Statista*. https://statista.com/statistics/272014/global-social-networks-ranked-by-number-of-users.
3. Dixon, S.J. (June 19, 2025b). Countries with the most Facebook users 2025. *Statista*. https://statista.com/statistics/268136/top-15-countries-based-on-number-of-facebook-users.
4. Gottfried, J. (January 31, 2024). *Americans' social media use. Pew Research Center*. https://pewresearch.org/internet/2024/01/31/americans-social-media-use.
5. LinkedIn Advertise. (n.d.-a). Why advertise on LinkedIn? https://business.linkedin.com/marketing-solutions/why-advertise-on-linkedin.
6. Maxwell, C. (December 4, 2020). Increasing social in a digital year. *Terrostar Interactive Media*. https://terrostar.com/increasing-social-in-a-digital-year.
7. Miller, J. & LinkedIn Marketing Solutions. (2017). The sophisticated marketer's guide to LinkedIn. *LinkedIn Corporation*. https://business.linkedin.com/content/dam/me/business/en-us/marketing-solutions/cx/2017/pdfs/Sophisticated-Marketers-Guide-to-LinkedIn-v03.12.pdf.
8. Dixon, S.J. (June 25, 2025c). LinkedIn: U.S. users 2025, by income. *Statista*. https://statista.com/statistics/1330852/linkedin-us-users-by-income.
9. Pew Research Center. (n.d.). Social media fact sheet. https://pewresearch.org/internet/fact-sheet/social-media/#who-uses-each-social-media-platform.
10. Richey, K. (August 3, 2016). Market to who matters with the LinkedIn Marketing Solutions Platform Overview [eBook]. *LinkedIn for Marketing Blog*. https://linkedin.com/business/marketing/blog/content-marketing/market-to-who-matters-with-the-linkedin-marketing-solutions-platform.
11. Graffius, S.M. (January 1, 2024). Lifespan (half-life) of social media posts: update for 2024. *ScottGraffius.com*. http://scottgraffius.com/blog/files/social-24.html.
12. Anderson, C.C. (March 26, 2025). *How long does a LinkedIn post ACTUALLY last? LinkedIn Corporation*. https://linkedin.com/pulse/how-long-does-linkedin-post-actually-last-chris-c-anderson-jtrwe.
13. Bellan, R. (September 25, 2020). Americans trust LinkedIn and Pinterest with data, but not Facebook. *Forbes*. https://forbes.com/sites/rebeccabellan/2020/09/25/americans-trust-linkedin-and-pinterest-with-data-but-not-facebook.

2. How LinkedIn Is Used Today for Business

1. Edelman. (n.d.). [Edelman Trust Barometer]. https://edelman.com/trust/trust-barometer

2. LinkedIn Premium. (n.d.). [Premium Career Features | LinkedIn Premium]. https://premium.linkedin.com/careers/career.

3. LinkedIn Advertise. (n.d.-b). [Advertise to LinkedIn's Audience of Professionals | LinkedIn Ads]. http://business.linkedin.com/marketing-solutions/audience.

4. Lybrand, S. (August 14, 2023). Employee branding: A guide to getting started. *LinkedIn Talent Blog.* https://linkedin.com/business/talent/blog/talent-acquisition/employer-branding.

3. Optimizing Your LinkedIn Profile for Maximum Impact

1. Fisher, C. (August 3, 2016). 5 steps to improve your LinkedIn profile in minutes. *LinkedIn Official Blog.* https://linkedin.com/blog/member/product/5-steps-to-improve-your-linkedin-profile-in-minutes.

2. St Louis, D. (2022, March 23). Are professional headshots important? [Video Report]. *HeadShots Inc.* https://headshots-inc.com/blog/do-business-headshots-really-matter.

3. Abbot, L. (August 1, 2024). 10 tips for taking a professional LinkedIn profile photo. *LinkedIn Talent Blog.* https://linkedin.com/business/talent/blog/product-tips/tips-for-taking-professional-linkedin-profile-pictures.

4. LinkedIn Help. (n.d.-a). Manage your public profile URL. https://linkedin.com/help/linkedin/answer/a542685/customizing-your-public-profile-url.

4. Build Your Network

1. LinkedIn Help. (n.d.-b). [Personalize invitations to connect | LinkedIn Help]. https://linkedin.com/help/linkedin/answer/a563153.

2. 2. Porter, G. (2013). *Your network is your net worth: Unlock the hidden power of connections for wealth, success, and happiness in the digital age.* Atria Books. My Book

7. LinkedIn for Business: Free vs. Paid

1. Hakami, S. (August 20, 2023). Does LinkedIn InMail (really) work for lead generation? *GTMnow.* https://gtmnow.com/linkedin-inmail.

2. Dixon, S.J. (June 25, 2025d). LinkedIn: global users 2019-2023, by subscription type. *Statista.* https://statista.com/statistics/1335947/linkedin-global-users-by-subscription.

8. Prospecting on LinkedIn: Finding and Connecting with Potential Clients

1. Note that LinkedIn currently does not show the number of results for a search, so this number comes from my last documented search in preparation for the first version of this book in August 2024.

2. LinkedIn Help. (n.d.-c). Types of restrictions for sending invitations. https://linkedin.com/help/linkedin/answer/a551012.
3. Summit Partners. (n.d.). *Not all buyers are ready to buy: How the 95:5 rule can refine your Go-to-Market Strategy.* https://summitpartners.com/resources/refine-your-go-to-market-strategy-95-5-rule.

9. Creating Content That Resonates on LinkedIn

1. Simmonds, R. (May 22, 2025). *50+ LinkedIn statistics marketers need to know in 2025. Foundation Marketing.* https://foundationinc.co/lab/b2b-marketing-linkedin-stats.
2. Woods, A. (2017–2025a). *The Content 10x Podcast.* https://content10x.com/podcast.
3. Woods, A. (September 10, 2020b). How to use influencer marketing effectively with Neal Schaffer. *The Content 10x Podcast.* https://content10x.com/how-to-use-influencer-marketing-effectively-with-neal-schaffer.

10. Leveraging AI to Enhance Your LinkedIn

1. Schaffer, N. (January 8, 2024a). 11 incredible AI LinkedIn headshot tools to create the perfect LinkedIn profile picture. *Neal Schaffer.* https://nealschaffer.com/ai-linkedin-headshot.

13. LinkedIn Case Studies: Real-World Success Stories

1. Schaffer, N. (2011d). Maximizing LinkedIn for sales and social media marketing: An unofficial, practical guide to selling & developing B2B business on LinkedIn. My Book
2. Schaffer, N. (2011e). Maximizing LinkedIn for sales and social Media marketing: An unofficial, practical guide to selling & developing B2B business on LinkedIn. My Book.
3. Maltseva, I. (February 13, 2025). LinkedIn is my #1 source of new clients as a consultant – Here's my exact process. *Buffer.* https://buffer.com/resources/linkedin-source-new-clients-consultant.
4. Neal, E. (May 2, 2025a). 12 success stories that prove personal branding on LinkedIn Works. *DSMN8.* https://dsmn8.com/blog/personal-branding-linkedin-success-stories.
5. Neal, E. (May 2, 2025b). 12 success stories that prove personal branding on LinkedIn Works. *DSMN8.* https://dsmn8.com/blog/personal-branding-linkedin-success-stories.
6. Samba, E. (April 21, 2025). How I built a $2.6 million Agency in year one without a sales team – Using nothing but LinkedIn. *HubSpot Blog.* https://blog.hubspot.com/marketing/linkedin-selling-and-authenticity.

7. Neal, E. (May 2, 2025c). 12 success stories that prove personal branding on LinkedIn Works. *DSMN8*. https://dsmn8.com/blog/personal-branding-linkedin-success-stories.

About the Author

Neal Schaffer didn't set out to become a LinkedIn expert. It just happened.

Back in 2008, while working in B2B sales, Neal saw something others missed: LinkedIn wasn't just a digital resume site—it was the future of professional relationship-building. Coming from a sales background, he understood networking in a way that most "social media experts" didn't. More importantly, his sales experience had given him a results-oriented work ethic that differed from the typical marketing and PR approaches of the time—he needed strategies that actually generated measurable outcomes, not just brand awareness.

So he started blogging about LinkedIn strategies that actually worked. One blog post led to another, then to his first book in 2009, then to speaking gigs around the world. Fifteen years later, Neal has spoken in more than a dozen countries across four continents, shared his insights with over 500 audiences, and authored multiple award-winning books, including *Digital Threads* and *The Age of Influence.*

But Neal's mission goes deeper than LinkedIn tactics. As a speaker, fractional CMO, consultant, and instructor at Rutgers Business School, UCLA Extension, and Solvay Brussels School Vietnam, he's worked with everyone from Fortune 50 companies to a Grammy Award-winning musician to fast-growing startups, and he's frustrated by watching companies waste money on inefficient marketing while ignoring what actually drives growth: smart and modern digital marketing strategies enhanced by genuine relationships with customers, employees, and content creators. "I see businesses throwing money at tactics that don't work while completely overlooking the fundamentals," Neal explains. "Smart marketing comes first—then relationships become the icing on the cake that amplifies everything."

Maybe it's in his DNA—his father was both an educator and an entrepreneur. Or maybe it's just who Neal is: someone who believes business success comes from smart fundamentals enhanced by authentic relationships, not shortcuts or quick fixes.

When he's not speaking on stage or teaching digital marketing, you'll find Neal in Irvine, California, where he lives with his wife and two children. He's fluent in Japanese and Mandarin Chinese, loves his L.A. sports teams, and can usually be found walking, jogging, playing pickleball, or hunting down the best food in whatever city he's visiting.

Neal's approach to digital marketing mirrors his approach to life: authentic, relationship-focused, and designed for the long game. Through his podcast, *Your Digital Marketing Coach*, his blog at https://nealschaffer.com, and his speaking and consulting work, Neal continues to help businesses cut through the noise and build real, sustainable success.

www.ingramcontent.com/pod-product-compliance
Lightning Source LLC
Chambersburg PA
CBHW071421210326
41597CB00020B/3596

* 9 7 9 8 9 9 4 0 7 7 9 0 0 *